# Treasures of the Soul

Dear Christie,

you are such a light
in my life! Wishing
much love + light!
Love,

*[signature]*

# Treasures of the Soul

### ... uncovering life's hidden lessons

Drusilla Burrough

Legwork Team Publishing
New York

*Legwork Team Publishing*
*80 Davids Drive, Suite One*
*Hauppauge, NY 11788*
*www.legworkteam.com*
*Phone: 631-944-6511*

*First Edition: 05/04/2012*

*Printed in the United States of America*
*This book is printed on acid-free paper*
*Designed by Gayle L. Newman*

### To my children,

who inspire me to remember that the only thing that is real is Love.

### To my husband,

who believes in me, loves me unconditionally and always encourages me to reach for my dreams.

### To my family,

for they are a constant reminder that I am loved simply because I exist.

### To my friends and clients,

who have taught me so much and have reflected back to me the truth that we are all one.

### To God, my guides and the angels,

for allowing me to be of service and urging me to do my part as a lightworker by bringing *Treasures of the Soul* to fruition.

### To me,

for having the courage to believe in my own magnificence, perseverance to never cease searching for truth, and faith to believe that I can accomplish whatever I set my mind to.

It is not about the adversities
or even the joys that present themselves in our lives,
but rather how we choose to respond to them,
learn from them and then uncover the hidden

*Treasures of the Soul.*

Drusilla Burrough

# Contents

# Contents

## SECTION FOUR: *Vehicle for Healing and Light*

## SECTION FIVE: *Moving On and More ...*

# Contents

# Foreword

By Janet Mulhall

*(Long Island, New York business owner
and healthcare practitioner for over twenty years)*

If the saying, "We are what we eat," is true then surely we become what we believe we are. The author has revealed her life story in a positive, thoughtful, open, and blameless book. She reveals her growth and transformation in such a soulful way that you are certain she is speaking directly to you.

She shares her "ordinary" life, her extraordinary journey through childhood, adulthood, motherhood, and finally "womanhood" as we watch her find the passion and joy of that gift. You will recognize her immediately. She is me, she is you, she is him, and she is us. She touches the reader, pulling on those invisible strings that connect us all.

She does not overanalyze, justify, or get lost in "could have" or "should have." She shows us how to lift our wings and simply move on.

She is a rebel, a compassionate warrior. She is a survivor sharing her shield. She whispers gently and at moments, shouts with passion to move us forward. She teaches us how to embrace and let go of the "junk" that blocks our life's path. This book will transform you. This book will inspire you. This book will remind you of what you knew from the moment you were born. You are a SOUL!

# Acknowledgments

*S*ince I have changed the names of family, friends, and clients, I cannot correctly name all of the people who helped and inspired me to make *Treasures of the Soul* a reality. However, you all know who you are. So without naming names, I will do my best to acknowledge everyone.

I offer thanks to my ex-husband who provided the catalyst for me to remember that I am special, lovable, magnificent, and worthy of having all of my dreams come true. Those whom we perceive to be our greatest adversaries often turn out to be our greatest teachers. He was the best.

To my son, for unintentionally helping me face my fear of abandonment and for teaching me the true meaning of unconditional love; I love you, my sweet baby boy.

To my daughters, thank you for putting up with my deep and constant quest for spiritual truth, and for listening to all of my "ah ha" moments, even when you had no idea what I was talking about. Thank you for just being you. I love you both.

To my loving, supportive husband, for your consistency, patience and gentle nature; when I am with you I feel cherished and adored. I feel respected and appreciated, and completely loved despite my faults and shortcomings. I adore you.

# Acknowledgments

To my mom, dad and eight siblings, you all inspire me with your ability to choose love, forgiveness, and goodness. I am so proud to be part of our family and this book is one way to tell you how much I love you.

To my writing teacher, over the years you provided a safe, loving and professional environment that allowed me to express myself and share my soul. You enabled me to grow as a writer and hone my craft under your unwavering support and positive direction. Thank you, also, to the numerous talented writers who shared their work in the many classes we took together. I learned so much from all of you.

To my clients, for allowing me to be part of your lives, even for just a moment, and for trusting me enough to share your hearts and souls with me so that I could share mine with you.

To my friends, who loved and supported me, though many times what I was saying or believed to be my truth made no sense to you at all; I could tell you had faith in me and trusted and loved me anyway, and it made all the difference.

I acknowledge the dedicated efforts of Yvonne Kamerling and Janet Yudewitz of Legwork Team Publishing. I extend my gratitude to them and their team of design, editorial and technical professionals, for transforming my manuscript into the book you hold in your hands.

# Introduction

*Treasures of the Soul* was born mostly out of intense adversity in my life but thankfully from joy as well. Just as birthing a child is agonizing but resulting in a miracle, so was the process I was asked to endure, in order to obtain such amazing understanding and inspiration to allow truth to emerge.

This book is about "my story." At times, it has been wonderful and terribly tragic, not unlike many human beings who choose to incarnate onto this beautiful planet. However, I am blessed with a strong faith, tremendous intuitiveness, and wonderful teachers who came into my life exactly when needed. I learned, through the principles they taught, that I am strong, beautiful, capable, and magnificent. I am loveable just the way I am and loving myself is the first step to becoming love. What I believe about myself and my world will create my life, so I have learned to think positive thoughts and embrace the magic of affirmation. My life changed dramatically because of this knowledge. I discovered that the answers to any questions that stir inside my heart lie within me. Through spiritual practices like prayer, meditation, journaling, and others, I uncovered enlightened truth and acquired a peace that had previously eluded me.

Like almost every other traveler on a true and noble spiritual path, once something is *remembered* through the wisdom of our eternal soul, we have an intense need to share our new understanding with others and be of service. I began this journey of service by becoming a licensed massage therapist in my early forties. Massage became a vehicle for me

# Introduction

to reach the souls of so many wonderful people and share all that I have learned. When I asked God to allow me to be of service, He "signed me up" and sent me many people who needed to be empowered and reminded of their own magnificence. Gifts of Spirit began to unfold, my sensitivity increased, and I spontaneously began doing spiritual readings for clients during massage treatments. What was also miraculous was that as I taught, I continued to learn. I listened to my soul and my guides as I spoke, or at times, they spoke through me. I was in awe of the process, humbled and so grateful. Along the way, my own painful wounds from the past began to fully heal.

Over the years, as I grew in my practice and raised my three children as a single mom, I continued to pursue my passion for writing. I have always believed that it was part of my path. My guides urged me to stay focused on my intentions. They assured me that what I had to offer was valuable and that they would work with me to help shape the project and bring it forth when the time was right. I followed their guidance and slowly began to visualize *Treasures of the Soul.*

This book is divided into five sections, *Following the Call, Roots, Breaking Away, Vehicle for Healing and Light,* and *Moving On and More....* All of the sections have an introduction preceding multiple stories and poems, each able to stand on its own, which is why there may be details that are occasionally repeated. This was planned: if you read a story or poem, and feel it relevant to someone you know, you can share it and they can read and understand it on its own. All five sections combined contain approximately sixty writings, each several pages long. In the *Introductions,* I ask you, the reader, to focus on certain things as you read each writing in that section. By following my suggestions and discovering what I learned from my own life experiences, it is my hope that you will journey inside your own life and do the same.

The underlying purpose of *Treasures of the Soul* is to teach that our stories may be different, but as human beings, no matter where we live or what our personal circumstances may be, we are all much more similar than we are different. Feelings of sadness, sorrow, heartache, loss, anger, hurt and longing as well as joy, love, compassion, and hope are universal. The lessons we learn during our time in the physical realm are common and collective. The main reasons we are here are to learn unconditional love and forgiveness for self and others, and to move beyond the illusion of duality and loneliness, into truth and unity. If I hurt you or if I show you love, I am doing the same for myself. There is no separation. Hidden within our experiences are the gemstones of wisdom and enlightenment that will allow us to radiate more divine light in the world in order to to finally triumph over the darkness. If you hear my story and you are overcome with emotions of any kind, you are deeply connected to me and I am more closely connected to you. We can teach, learn, and share with each other through love and compassion. One of the most important things for all of us sharing the physical journey is that we learn our lessons through our experiences. In doing so, we will not continue to draw into our life new and painful circumstances that carry with them the same unlearned lessons.

*Following the Call* is about finding one's life purpose by looking for the clues from our childhood and utilizing tools such as prayer, meditation, visualization, and seeking spiritual guidance. We can then remember the vows we made to our soul, our guides, and to God about why we chose to make this earthly pilgrimage once again. It is much shorter than the other four, but I thought it was important to help the reader think about and uncover his or her own life purpose—what gift or gifts he or she intended

# Introduction

to give the world. As with every story or poem in this book, at the end are several lines highlighting what I took with me from the experience. I reveal what I learned and the beautiful gemstone of wisdom and enlightenment I was able to place carefully into the spaces of my heart. This process enables my soul to shine more brilliantly and helps me move closer to truly becoming Love. It is a process that can do the same for you.

*Roots* is my journey through my own childhood. It is my unique story growing up in a family with eight children, a stay-at-home mom and a working dad in the 1950s and '60s. There is confusion, loneliness, joy, faith, pride, and lots of craziness. The stories are entertaining, adventure-filled, chaotic, and nostalgic. What is the same are similar feelings and emotions we all feel as children learning to find our way in the world. It also begins to provide clues about how my childhood and perception of myself and my life propelled me to make my choices as an adult. Throughout this book, as I tell you about my life, I change the names of my family, and others to protect privacy and ensure that this work would not wound anyone, even my ex-husband. It was never my intention to hurt him or any of his family.

*Breaking Away* is about the period in my life when I moved beyond my childhood out into the world. This section is painful and tragic for me. I entered into a marriage that was never good for me. Yet, I chose my first husband for a reason. I explore my reasons for this choice. How did I see myself and my world that allowed me to draw into my life a relationship that caused me more sadness than joy? This section also includes the miraculous birth of my three children. I share the love I feel for them and how they suffered, as well, from the disharmony in my marriage. Most important, however, is that although this is the most difficult time in my life, it provided me with the most beautiful of all *gemstones*. It was the catalyst that allowed me to remember how wonderful and loving I am. Our greatest adversaries and our most dysfunctional and painful relationships are often our greatest teachers. I emerged from this time with a new awareness and a remembrance of who I have always been: a divine being of love and light.

*Vehicle for Healing and Light* is filled with miraculous stories of my work as a massage therapist and a spiritual teacher. In 1997, when I began practicing massage, I was still broken and traumatized from the long divorce and custody battle that had just ended. I wondered how I would be able to raise my three children alone and still have enough energy for my clients. I quickly learned that God doesn't ask us to come to Him when we "fix" all of our problems; he says, "Come to me with all of your pain and dysfunction because you are perfect for the work I need you to do." As I continued to offer my prayer each day, to be of service in the world, miracle upon miracle began to occur in my treatment room. Healings happened on many levels. Lost souls, unable to make their way on their paths, awakened, and began following their bliss and remembering their own magnificence. In healing others, my own healing progressed. In this section I share some of those stories. Again, I have changed all of the names and a few details on occasion, to protect their privacy, but the stories are true and the miracles are amazing.

*Moving On and More* ... follows my journey as my children grow to be adults. They had their share of difficulty. They struggled with understanding and processing their confusing childhoods. I tried to teach them spiritual principles I learned, but mostly I simply loved them unconditionally. There were some triumphant and joyful moments and some sad ones as they tried to find their way. During this time, I attracted into my life, a loving, kind, and generous man who would eventually become my husband, because I had learned to love myself and fully believed I was worthy of that kind of love. My parents grew old and my dad passed away. Just like every other part of my life, there were and still are joys and sorrows, good times, and not so good. However, at this stage, I continue to remember that there are no coincidences in life. Everything happens for a reason and every person who crosses my path does so in order for me to learn, to teach, or both. I embrace the adversity as well as the joy from the beginning through the end. I look deeply and openly for answers and lessons and stay in humble gratitude for all life brings my way. This section covers approximately the last ten years and is the present ongoing and unfolding of my incredible life.

The most exciting part of this book project for me is its possible longevity and potential to reach across oceans and hopefully touch the lives of people from every nation and culture. I believe that if we can focus more on our similarities rather than our differences, we will all be more tolerant, compassionate, empathetic, and peaceful toward one another. Again, what binds us together as one human family is our need to love and be loved. We struggle with the ever-needy ego that always "wants to want more than it wants to have." Out of that need to have more or want what others have, arise emotions such as jealousy, hatred, fear, intolerance, and vengeance. Learning to embrace our adversities, peel away layers of pain, anger, heartache, sadness, or whatever feelings and emotions obscure the truth buried within them, helps us learn our lessons. We not only learn the reason why we drew an experience into our life, but in going deeply into the center and asking the question, "How can this experience allow me to be better, more loving, wise, compassionate, and more divine?" we emerge as a being much more aligned with our soul's light. Blame, guilt and self-pity fall by the wayside as we bask in that new and radiant light. Each time we connect with this process and find awareness, understanding, wisdom, and truth, we discover we no longer attract that lesson into our life. We begin to grow through joy rather than adversity, most of the time.

I ask you, my new friends and fellow travelers, to send me your stories if you wish. However, I ask you also to challenge yourself to return to your past or embrace your present. As you tell your story, I urge you to try to think deeply about how your experience changed you. Has it helped you to become more loving or are you holding on to anger, resentment or other negative emotions? If the latter is true, how can you see your experience differently? What was or what is your life, your soul, and God trying to teach you that you refuse or are unable to learn, and thus continue to experience pain and suffering? At the end of your stories, just as I have, I ask you to share your own wisdom, truth, and light as you reveal your personal, yet common emotions and feelings.

With your permission, of course, I will then put these stories together in a new book and hopefully more and more books as we all come together in order help and heal each other. It is my goal and my dream that through this work, I, we, can do our part in bringing more tolerance, understanding, compassion, forgiveness, unity, and most of all love into the world. I know, from my own individual story of adversity and how I overcame it, that it has helped give courage, strength, and hope to many people who had been experiencing comparable things or merely similar emotions. Let us all unite together and offer to each other the gifts of love, light, truth and peace!

## Namaste,
*(I honor the divinity within you)*

## Drusilla

# Following the Call

# Introduction to Following the Call

This first section is rather small in comparison to the rest but I felt it was necessary. We all struggle with remembering and defining what our life purpose is here on earth. It is difficult and some people spend an entire lifetime searching, never truly feeling as if they have found it. I believe that the clues to unlocking this mystery lie both in our soul's eternal memory but also in the remembrances of our childhoods. If we take the time to look back to that period of innocence and youth, and at the same time ask for spiritual guidance, we will find the answers.

Think back to that precious and sacred time. Remember what it was that made you light up inside. Was it drawing and creating beautiful works of art with crayons, paints, or colored pencils? Did you love to sing, spend hours in front of a mirror with a hair brush held up to your mouth like a microphone, and imagine sharing your gift with the world? Perhaps you saw or heard about the senseless killing of animals for their fur and it ignited a fury and a determination to stop such injustices. I assure you, there was *something* that brought forth your "bliss," and all you need to discover it, is a sincere intention and a prayer for the assistance from Spirit.

For me, it was writing as well as a desire to be of service to God and my fellow human beings. As you will see from the few pieces in this section, my dreams were born early in my life and they never died. At times they were put on a back burner as I struggled through the adversities and challenges in my life. Yet, they were never far from my consciousness and my writing always provided an outlet for my feelings and my confusion about my life here on earth.

The clues, for you, may also lie in a memory of a certain person who recognized something in you that was special, unique, and different; someone who saw your talent, perhaps even before you did. So explore, too, your relationships during your childhood. There is nothing more gratifying than the feeling that your life means something, because it absolutely does. We all long to leave this place a little better than when we came here and we all have the unique and individual gifts in order to do so.

I hope you enjoy these stories and poems that tell about how I discovered my own life purpose. Some writings in this section reveal how I struggled at times to remain on my destined path and the tools, insights, and wisdom I discovered along the way.

As you read or when you are finished reading, allow the images of your own childhood to float spontaneously into your mind. Let them reveal to you the clues that will unlock your own life purpose and thus, the remembrance of your soul. Begin to fill your journal with your own *Treasures of the Soul*.

*This poem illustrates my process of choosing to move from the spirit world to the earth plane. This natural progression, I believe, occurs in the state of "life between life."*

# Illusion of Change

I cannot see, how can it be
I challenge to my God,
That my giant soul that has no end
Will fit into that tiny pod.

In a moment of faith, I take the leap
Crossing over from heaven to earth.
I enter a warm and watery womb
Where I await my miraculous birth.

This dark soft place has a rhythmic beat,
Consistent, comforting, and calm.
It mixes with a swooshing, swishing sound
That makes me feel there is love all around.

Each day is different, each day is the same
As I am and yet I am not.
I am still the spirit who was born of Love
Being human doesn't change that a lot.

Tiny fingers move and a mouth suckles same,
And they grow and evolve into me.
I have always been and will always remain,
Yet appearing different from the biology I see.

Though hesitant to leave, I am thrust into life;
I thrash and I scream and reach high.
I look for the arms of the voice soft and sweet
That I know will hold me tight while I cry.

My spirit is wise coming to love and to teach
As a child few will acknowledge such.
Often children's power goes unrecognized here,
Yet they bring light through their love and their touch.

Today there is change to the consciousness of man;
The veil between two worlds grows thin.
We remember we are spirit and always will be
And we find heaven not without but within.

Whether infant, child, adult or the aged,
We are souls who evolve and grow.
We are connected to all, and hear the same voice;
God's words reveal all we should know.

So we listen to children as keenly as the wise sage,
For they are truly one and the same.
In the end, when the blessed human form dissolves,
We carry love back to from whence we all came.

"LIFE IS A CONTINUOUS JOURNEY
OF DEATH AND REBIRTH
BOTH IN THE PHYSICAL WORLD
AND IN SPIRIT.
WE NEVER CEASE TO EXIST.
WE GROW, CHANGE AND REMEMBER
OUR AUTHENTICITY—OUR
MAGNIFICENT SOUL."

# *Whispering Waves*

*W*here does it begin and where does it end? Somewhere out in the vastness it arises—a tiny swell, perhaps, having originated in response to an unknown urging. So begins its journey racing toward the shore, unaware of its reason for being or purpose for existing, only that it was born and instinctively knows it must move forward. Lapping, churning, crossing paths with fellow travelers, it continues. Creatures large and small glide along and beneath the rising swell as it gathers strength edging ever closer to its destination. With one final explosion of power and hidden purpose it crashes wildly, pounding the earth in triumph proclaiming, "I am here! I have arrived." In one thunderous moment all of its energy and reason for being are gone. It is pulled back into the vastness. Its complexity and uniqueness are diffused, separated, fragmented … gone!

So, I sit at the water's edge, at the dawning of a new day. The early September sun struggles to bring warmth even as the anxious autumn chill tries urgently to regain its hold. I am alone in the peaceful solitude. Only the sounds of the waves and the squeals of the graceful gulls break the silence. The previous, agonizing night offered little rest as I tried unsuccessfully to quiet my troubled mind. In the darkness of the early morn I surrendered to the elusive veil of slumbering consciousness, accepting that it was not to be. I find myself drawn here to this loving, watery womb hoping to find the peace and tranquility for which I so desperately long. Searching for answers that I have sought countless times, I find those answers that sadly have a limited lifespan within my awareness, and I weep. Soft tears give way to gut-wrenching sobs filled with a profound sadness and sorrow. These powerful, painful emotions are perplexing as they are in conflict with the contentment and the joy that fills my heart and mind when I contemplate the richness and beauty of my present life. I allow the process to unfold as an inner voice tenderly assures me that what I am experiencing is necessary in order to release even more of the pain and darkness that still lies buried deep in the recesses of my otherwise illumined soul. Fasting for many days, as I have been doing, not only purges physical toxins but the emotional ones as well. As always, change occurs rapidly in my life. I have requested this path and yet many times I resist the changes and I struggle against the shifting, blowing, blinding sands of life.

I feel, many times, like each and every one of those rolling arms of the sea, racing to my destination never quite knowing for sure exactly what absolute and complete purpose I have come to accomplish. Lifetime after lifetime I race to the ethereal shore, only to be pulled back into the vastness of the cosmic infinity which diffuses the complexity and uniqueness of who I had been—only to, again and again, give birth to a being quite different and yet exactly the same.

Gazing upon the miles and miles of open sea, being engulfed by the endless muffled pounding of the surf, I am overwhelmed with emotions; sadness, sorrow, grief, gratitude, and hope rise and fall with the incoming surf. As I move more deeply into the scene before me I realize that today, *I am as the wave powering unstoppable toward the expansive shore,* knowing that when I arrive it will be a mere signal, a sign that this phase of my life is over. I will be pulled back into the eternity of my inner world, always and forever pregnant with brilliant insights, awesome creativity, divine inspiration, and renewed purpose. I will carefully gather, from that space, the gifts of wisdom, love, and illumination so that I may continue my journey here. I will then begin to build and grow in strength, determination, and purpose once again. Yet, this time I vow to slow down, expand my energy outward and upward. Each and every moment I will choose to stay fully present and enjoy the incredible journey. I will revel in our world filled with a myriad of colors, sights, sounds, emotions, triumphs and defeats, as well as in a glorious knowing that I am exactly where I am supposed to be at any given moment—the destination—irrelevant!

"IN ORDER TO CONTINUOUSLY
GROW AND RECEIVE
DIVINE WISDOM AND TRUTH
I MUST ALWAYS REMEMBER
TO RELEASE OR GIVE AWAY THAT
WHICH NO LONGER SERVES ME!"

"LIFE HERE ON THE EARTH PLANE
IS FILLED WITH MANY
DEATHS AND REBIRTHS,
AND ENDLESS OPPORTUNITIES
TO REALIZE OUR DREAMS."

# *Clues Come from the Write Place*

"Mom, Mom, guess what? I wrote a story, a real story all by myself," I announced excitedly as I waved a sheet of lined yellow paper in front of my mom's face.

I was only four years old so I knew this was a really big deal for a kid my age. I felt so proud and was certain it was a masterpiece. I couldn't wait for my mom to read it.

"OK, OK, Mom responded in her quiet, gentle way. Just give me a minute and I'll take a look."

Mom finished up folding the laundry and then sat down holding my amazing story in her hands. I couldn't wait for her to finish so she could tell me how wonderful it was and how she couldn't believe I had written it all by myself. I shifted back and forth in my seat watching her face as she read. She didn't have much expression, and as a matter of fact, she looked a bit confused as she moved her attention from the piece of yellow paper smudged with graphite to my anxious little face.

When she was finished she lifted her head and began to give me some well thought out criticism. I don't remember at all what it was. The only thing I remember was that I was crushed. How could she not see that my story was unbelievably good? It was exciting and full of adventure about a little boy and girl who triumphed over all kinds of terrible things only to live happily ever after in the end. Mom was kind and loving as she delivered her advice but I could only feel hurt and anger when she didn't think I was the best writer in the entire world.

Nevertheless, her inability to see my gift didn't deter me. That time long ago when I was only four years old, was the first time I knew that

# Treasures of the Soul

I was a writer. I loved to write. Over the years I journaled, wrote short stories, and poems. In the back of my mind I always heard a still small voice telling me that writing would be part of my life's work. I believed that with all my heart. I didn't know what I would write or why my work would be of value, but I knew I was born to write. However, I never forgot about my first story, and being that my mom was such a good writer herself, I still didn't understand why she didn't appreciate my gift the way I did when I shared it with her.

Many years later, when I was in high school, my mom called me into her bedroom. She pulled open a drawer in her desk and took out an old piece of yellow paper carefully folded in half and she handed it to me. To my surprise, it was the story I had written all those years ago. Mom had kept it!

"So she did think it was great! I was wrong," I thought, feeling relieved and overjoyed.

As I unfolded the paper and scanned the fading gray pencil marks that were my first attempt at writing, I was stunned! There was not one legible word on the page. I didn't know how to read or write at that time. There were a lot of letters all put together to look like words, but they weren't words at all. It looked like a foreign language. In my head, I remembered so clearly that I knew exactly what I wanted to say, but I guess I just pretended that I knew how to write and believed that my mom would understand. Obviously, she didn't, but she never said a word to discourage me. I guess she just tried the best she could to make me believe that I had, indeed, written my very first story.

"Wow," I blurted out with complete surprise. "You saved it. I can't believe you saved it all these years. But Mom, it doesn't say anything, not even one real word. Why didn't you tell me?"

"I really didn't know what to tell you at the time, Dru. I could see how excited you were so I tried to give you some help as if it really was a legible story. But it was hard since I didn't even know what it said."

I finally understood and I was grateful for my mom's kindness and compassion. However, that memory, I realized, was probably the only memory I had of that time when I was four years old. I never forgot that day. I never forgot how I felt and how excited I was. Years later when I began to search for clues about what my life's purpose was, that moment, that story always came to my mind. I knew, even then at such a tender young age, that I was born to write. That was my clue. That was my answer and it gave me the confidence and the motivation to pursue the dream that my little four-year-old self had unleashed on that very memorable day, so long ago.

> "THE CLUES TO MY LIFE PURPOSE,
> TOOK UP RESIDENCE IN MY
> CHILDHOOD MEMORIES.
> ONCE I JOURNEYED BACK TO THAT
> TIME, I FOUND MY BLISS, AND
> I FOLLOWED MY PATH."

This poem is about meditation. Through this spiritual practice, I have experienced a world that cannot be perceived through the five senses. Meditation brings me into complete communion with God. It is here that he speaks to me in the silence, in the space between my thoughts. It is here that I know God's unconditional love for me. It is also here where I can remember the promises I made to myself and God about what I wanted to accomplish while here on earth.

## To Be

To explore the world that rests within
Requires little thought.
For in the space between the words
Lies all that can be taught.

To view a place that can't be touched
By probing, human hands,
Necessitates a silent time
To travel foreign lands.

To die while we are still alive
Teaches us how to live.
Melting away the spiritual veil
Allows us to forgive.

To hold a vision of perfect love
Helps memories return.
We see within the hearts of man
The goodness we discern.
To imprison souls that long for light
In caverns in our core
Leaves us empty, unfulfilled,
Never finding heaven's door.

To pray for insight, answers, truth
Brings music filled with hope.
Hidden in notes of celestial song
Are tools we need to cope.

To serve each other with selfless love
Is all we need to shine.
What we do for those in need
We do for the Divine.

To mollify our troubled selves
That searches far for God,
Angels whisper "look within"
Smiling softly, with a nod.

To blossom from seed to lovely flower
Requires a grateful heart.
We never need return to God
We were never really apart.

To answer the question "Who am I?"
We must question "Who are you?"
One light exists connecting all.
One being reveals the truth.

To walk our walk and talk our talk
Must always be our prayer.
In the end, we pass beyond
And our legacy, we share.

"MANY TIMES, TO FIND
THE ANSWERS TO THE DEEP
MEANINGFUL QUESTIONS IN LIFE
REQUIRES SIMPLY "BEING"
NOT "DOING."
FOR, IN THE SILENCE AND
THE STILLNESS LIES THE TRUTH—
GOD'S TRUTH!"

The year that my first child Jake was born seemed be a time for dreams to be remembered and reborn and for miracles to come true. I continued to write consistently. I believe this inspiration came from the tiny life growing inside of me, reminding me of a sacred contract I made about my life's purpose even before I was born. Vision is a piece that reveals that place of inspiration or "being in spirit" and it inspired to me to follow my dreams.

## Vision

To have a dream is not enough,
A voice within me cries.
You must, a vision, always have,
One seen, but through your eyes.

For dreams are seeds from heaven's realm
Sent down to be your tool.
Plant them well with sturdy roots
And let your vision be their food.

And then with faith that never wavers,
From seeds a burst of life,
With love and hope a flower blooms
To show your trial and strife.

Your dreams no longer rest within,
But live among the stars
Because a vision, you did have,
And freed them from your heart's bars.

"THE WAY TO
MANIFEST MY DREAMS
IS TO UTILIZE VISUALIZATION,
EMBRACE FAITH,
STAY IN GRATITUDE,
THEN TAKE ACTION!"

## SECTION TWO

# Roots

# Introduction to Roots

*W*riting about my childhood and my adolescence was difficult for me, mostly because my memory of that time is vague. I'm not sure exactly why, but I have determined through much inner work, that as a child, I felt life here on the earth plane was a scary place. I didn't understand why I felt as if I didn't really belong, even though I had a family that loved me very much. Even my name seemed foreign. When people would call me Drusilla, I wanted to say, "No that isn't my name." Yet, I didn't know why. It wasn't that I didn't like my name, it was just simply that Drusilla didn't seem to fit. I have often wondered: perhaps, when things got too confusing, I journeyed outside of my body and returned to the spirit world, my true home, leaving behind my physical form to operate rather unconsciously. So, I don't have a lot of clear memories from my childhood but I do have some of the important ones, and I have my seven brothers and sisters to fill in a lot of the gaps.

When I was very young, even as young as five or six, I seemed to know things. I seemed to be very wise about things that a child of that age should not know. I was raised in a very Catholic home and yet I always knew there was something missing for me within those teachings. I tried really hard to conform and accept my label as a "good Catholic girl" but there was always a force, an energy pulling me in a direction away from the Catholic teachings onto the path that was less confining—one that, today, defines my life. I didn't entirely reject Catholicism; I simply began to study other ways and methods of finding truth. I came to understand that spirituality, for me, brings to mind a giant sphere. That sphere includes organized religion, but it is not defined by any one set of beliefs or practices. There is only one God and one truth; yet, there are many paths we may choose in our quest for that truth.

As a child, when other children told me their problems, I was able to hear things that they didn't tell me, things they may not have known themselves. I received information that revealed the reason for their pain and confusion and what they needed to focus on in order for them to understand their experience and find their answers. I never questioned the process and never hesitated to say what came into my mind. Friends began to come to me for insight and inspiration, and I gave it with innocence and a deep desire to help others.

When I entered young adulthood, before I had any real adult experiences or boy-girl relationships, I found adults much older than I began coming to me for advice. Married women asked me about problems in their marriage, and somehow I knew what I was supposed to tell them so they could find their answers. The information always seemed to come so naturally and easily. Again, I didn't question it. I just gave whatever I received.

So why was I unable to find those answers for myself and for my own life? Why, as a young adult, did I make choices that took me down a path leading to much pain and heartache? Why did I see myself and my world in a way that kept me from loving myself and believing that I was worthy of love? I had a family and friends who did love me, but I was unable to receive that love and embrace it. Finding these answers has been one of the greatest challenges for me in my life: to understand my soul, my childhood, and to discover all the reasons that led to certain choices. Understanding this part of my life was the key that allowed me to ultimately remember who I have always been since the moment God created me many lifetimes ago. I was able to remember my divine nature and the purpose for which I decided to return to this beautiful earth.

Roots will take you on a journey through my own personal history. I think you will find many of the stories both entertaining and heartwarming. As you read about my story, again try to see yourself in my emotions and feelings. How does your own story relate to mine, not in exact content of course, but in the kind of adversity I was asked to face and the lessons I, in turn, needed to learn. Journey back to your own childhood! Discover how your own personal set of circumstances shaped your personality either revealing your soul and its purpose, or perhaps, obscuring it and making it hard for you to remember who you are and why you came here. Take some time and write about your most significant memories; then let your soul reveal the wisdom and insight meant to come through as a result of it. Allow your past to liberate you and set you free. You need no longer be imprisoned by memories that may have created an illusion, not the truth. See your past like a giant puzzle with many of the hidden pieces buried in the deepest most sacred recesses of your divine soul. Ask for spiritual guidance. Enlist the help of your guides and your angels to help you find those pieces, so that you can see the bigger picture and thus begin to truly remember your magnificence and your divine perfection.

*Treasures of the Soul*

When I was born in 1954, Mom already had a three- and a two-year-old at home. During her pregnancy she was very ill with serious ear infections. She turned to her mom and dad for help and they refused. In a meditation, as an adult, I journeyed into my mother's womb. I remembered knowing what she was going through. My spirit was able to travel outside of my tiny fetus to be there with her and comfort her. This poem was born after that meditation.

## Conversation with Mom at My Birth
*(Me to Mom)*

You thought I couldn't hear you
As you cried your anguished tears.
You felt since I couldn't see you
I'd be protected from your fears.

My sisters Sue and Kelly were small;
They required so much care.
But you had no strength and felt afraid;
You need to know, I was aware.

I sat beside you as you clutched your ears
So filled with illness and pain.
I stroked your head and held your hand
When your mom and dad never came.

You needed help and somehow you thought
That for once they'd be there for you.
They were way too busy, as they always were
And you screamed, "God, what will I do?"

"I just don't know how to do this;
I don't know how good mothers behave."
But Mom, kids depend on their parents;
You needed a love they never gave.

Even though I was growing inside you,
I could still see and hear and speak.
Remember when I whispered, "I love you
And I can't wait till we finally meet."

*(Mom to Me)*
My sweet baby I am sorry you suffered;
I didn't know you could feel my distress.
Now that you're here and safe in my arms,
I know God will take care of the rest.

It's true I don't have all the answers
But I promise I will always be there.
When your dad and I don't know what to do,
We'll ask God to answer our prayers.

Those prayers will be simply that He show us
How to help you feel loved and secure.
We're not quite sure how we'll do that
But we will, of that we are sure.

Thank you for choosing to come here
And allowing me to be your mom.
As I look in your eyes, I see wisdom and light,
And I feel peaceful, tranquil, and calm.

Just remember, Dru, not to take on my pain.
Separate what is mine and what's yours.
I sense, over time, you may hold it inside.
If you do, you'll create even more.

But I have faith in the strength of your spirit
To overcome all adversity and strife.
Your soul will rise up and you'll fly like the wind
As you live fully, your incredible life.

"THE RELATIONSHIP
BETWEEN A MOTHER AND A CHILD
BEGINS MUCH EARLIER
THAN THE MOMENT A CHILD ENTERS
THE PHYSICAL WORLD.
PERHAPS, IT BEGAN
MANY LIFETIMES AGO.
KNOWING THIS HELPED ME
TO NURTURE MY RELATIONSHIP
WITH MY OWN CHILDREN
AS THEY GREW SLOWLY
AND MIRACULOUSLY INSIDE OF ME.
I FELT AS IF
I ALREADY KNEW THEN."

## Company "B"

*D*ecember 15, 1963, 5:00 a.m.—I pull the covers up to my chin and snuggle deeper to stay warm. No light yet shines through the dark, cold windows. I wish I could go back to sleep. I can't. I hear those familiar footsteps coming up the stairs.

"God, how I wish he would oversleep just one time."

Then I hear the snapping of his fingers and his deep voice, "Rise and shine Company 'B!'" So we do, like six obedient, little soldiers. We tumble out of bed, fight over the bathroom, don our military-looking uniforms and head out the door into the frigid December morning.

No one speaks in the car. It's too darn early. The only audible sound is the continuous yawning as we shiver, praying that the heat will finally kick in.

"None of our friends are put through this every morning," I argue with myself in the privacy of my own mind.

There was no arguing with him, though. Dad made the rules and we followed. We pull into the parking lot. The ornate-looking dome on the top of the church towers above us, and one by one we file through the door and into the pew behind my father. My mom stayed home with the babies in those early years. Mass begins. We all know every movement and every word despite the fact that it is said in Latin. I feel an odd sense of comfort, like coming home again. I feel safe and protected, but let's be serious, at nine years old, my first choice would have been my cozy, warm bed.

So our day begins in the usual way and continues on to St. Agnes's Catholic Elementary School. I walk into my classroom and on the board is a beautiful Christmas tree drawn in green chalk. We sit down at our dark brown, pencil-rutted, wooden desks, and Sister Augustine announces her daily call.

"Anyone who went to mass this morning may go up and draw a candle on our tree."

All eyes turn to me as they know, of course, it would again be only me who rises. Thank goodness or else our poor little tree would be barren. I feel a sense of pride in my family as I meticulously draw a representation of our holy act of love and reverence.

School's out now. It's 8:00 p.m. Dinner's done. Everyone is bathed, babies are slathered in fragrant Johnson's baby lotion, everyone is in PJ's ready for the close of another day, and again I wait, hoping against hope that Dad will forget. Not likely!

Dad calls, "Rosary time!"

From four corners of the house we all grab our rosaries and gather in the living room; Mom, Dad and kids. We kneel down in front of a statue of the Sacred Heart of Jesus that has been carefully placed in a triangular shaped alcove, just above a six foot long indoor garden, about a foot high, spanning the entire length of the wall. I guess you could say, it is our sacred place, our domestic alter. The fact that occasional turtles, fish and hamsters are buried beneath the rich fertile soil that grows the many varieties of plants in the garden, only adds to its symbolic representation of continuous life. We say the rosary every night. It takes exactly fourteen minutes if you say it really fast and we try. However, Dad sets the pace, as he says the first part of the Our Father and Hail Mary and we say the second. We must kneel straight up and erect and if we dare to sit back on our heels, Dad gives "the look" and we shoot back up into position. One night, my sister Susan decided that we should suffer more as Jesus did, so we had to say the entire rosary with our arms extended out to our sides.

I'm sure we scored some big points in heaven with that one.

9:30 p.m.—I'm lying in my nice warm bed again saying my prayers. It's always the same every night. Besides being sorry for everything I can think of that I did wrong, like fighting with my siblings, telling little fibs (or sometimes big ones), and blessing everyone in my life, I say that one special prayer.

Even at nine years old, I pray "Dear God, please let me serve you."

I have no idea how I am going to do that, but I somehow know that there is a bright light deep inside of me. It has a voice that comes from somewhere beyond this world and urges me to bring that light out into this one. Sounds "hokey," I know, but I was never a "normal" child. I close my eyes, bring my small hand to my lips, and in a sincere and innocent gesture of adoration, blow a kiss to God up into the far away heavens and whisper, "Good night, I love you."

May 28, 2011—I am now fifty-seven years old. My dad passed away over eight years ago and he took with him his deep unwavering faith. Yet, for each of his eight children, he left behind tender, peaceful, and sometimes slightly annoying memories. Today those reminiscences allow each of us to share the thread of love and faith we learned in our youth. It weaves its way, continuously, into the tapestry of our adult lives. I have since gone beyond the confines of organized religion. There's too much judgment, intolerance, and violence for me. It seems to me that the dogma and doctrine of the various religions cause this separation and intolerance. Yet, if we peel it all away, like the layers of an onion, we find at the core of all religions one theme; love, forgiveness, and unity. I now find my truth everywhere. Nature has become my sacred alter. I hear truth floating on a gentle summer breeze or in the melodic song of a tiny whippoorwill. I find God in everyone for I feel we are all connected by one beautiful and loving energy. If I look deeply enough inside of you, I will find me. So I choose to honor the divinity and light inside of every human being, even when they are less than kind or loving to me. For, I believe, if they were in touch with that part of themselves that is perfect and divine, they could not behave in an unkind way. So, I choose to focus on the part of them that *is* perfect and divine and practice forgiveness. It's not easy sometimes, but I understand that forgiveness is more for *my* soul than for theirs.

I still struggle with my ever persistent ego that tries desperately to have me identify with anything or anyone in the physical world, so that it can remain in control. However, my consciousness and awareness—my soul, who I truly am—is stronger now. This allows me to be gentler with myself knowing that I am human as well as divine. If I make mistakes I try to forgive myself and move on.

Therefore, the theme of my life has not changed. The structure of my faith has not changed. It is still based on love, forgiveness, and unity. Perhaps it is merely the content within the structure that has changed— the way in which I find my truth, leaving my intentions steadfast and everlasting. I cherish my childhood and I am proud to be a member of such an incredible team, my family. Each of my siblings is beautiful, wise and compassionate. My mother continues to be an inspiration as she emits glorious love and light and is always smiling even when things are tough for her. She chooses to focus on all that is good in her life and I have received that precious gift from her. We, my brothers, sisters and I, are all who we are because of our somewhat odd childhood. I, for one, wouldn't trade it for anything.

We are **Company "B."**

"B"urrough.

"My parents' constant, unwavering dedication and commitment to their faith laid a strong spiritual foundation leading me to explore my own spiritual path. It also gave me the strength to endure the many adversities in my life, knowing I am not alone, ever."

# The "Gathering" of Memories

"No singing at the dinner table!" commanded my dad in his strong, forceful voice.

Those words still echo hauntingly in my mind, even though I haven't heard them in more than thirty years. As a child, this rule was simply the norm, and we never questioned it. Today, however, it seems very strange to me. You would think eight children singing happily through a meal would be a pleasant experience; but not to Dad. Eating while singing at the same time was not proper and definitely violated another hard and fast rule in our home: "don't talk (or sing) with your mouth full."

My childhood home was a maroon-colored split level on the South Shore of Long Island. We eventually added a third floor extension as our family continued to grow. There was a huge wooded property in the backyard with many white birch trees and a grey canvas hammock that hung lazily between two large oak trees. My siblings and I never really lay down peacefully in that hammock. Instead, we would wrap each other up in it and then spin it around in circles to see if the trapped victim would fall out. My sister, Marianna, did and broke her collar bone so that was the end of that game. Strategically placed in a row in the center of the yard were lots of bushes that had small purple flowers. When new buds bloomed, we would squeeze them between our fingers and they made a cool popping sound. Dad loved planting and enjoying his flowers, plants, and bushes so I'm sure he would not have been happy if he knew. Oh well, we couldn't be good Catholic kids all the time. In the front of the house was a massive weeping willow tree whose branches hung down all the way to the ground providing a perfect, well-concealed fort for our secret fantasies and imaginary adventures. There was a stoop (do they still call it that?). It was a small set of steps that led to the front door and there was a large bay window in the front of the house that was always adorned with festive decorations for every holiday. Inside our middle-class, domestic palace, there was always a pretty chaotic scene. It would never be described as very tidy and organized. Yet, there was a great feeling of safety and comfort that I felt as I retreated from my everyday activities like school, dance lessons, and kickball in the street. Fun, memorable games of "red light, green light, one, two, three," "hide and seek," and "Simon says," were all played on the front lawn.

My favorite room in our house was the dining room. It was located catty-corner to the living room and kitchen, and its windows faced the backyard. It wasn't at all fancy, just practical. The only thing in the room was a sturdy, colonial-looking oak table that stretched the entire length. On each end of the table were two armchairs where my mom and dad sat as king and queen of their domain. On either side of the table there were two long benches that accommodated all eight children: six girls and two boys. Hanging on the wall was a narrow wooden plank that Dad had stained with a light oak color. Together, as a family we created a map of Long Island on the plank using white, sea-polished stones we had collected at Fire Island and other Long Island beaches. That Burrough work of art still finds a home at my mom's house in Florida, hanging proudly and reminding us all of our roots.

Each night when I was growing up, we would all set the table together, well at least the older kids, anyway. One person did plates, others silverware and another water glasses.

"Dinner is ready," my mom would announce, like clockwork at 5:30 p.m. every day just as my dad arrived home from work.

All activity stopped and we all filed into the dining room and took our predetermined spots. I don't have any idea how those spots were originally decided upon. However, there was an occasional renegotiating of positions when someone would announce something like "I'm not sitting next to him, he chews too loud." After all, what could be more annoying? What especially bothered me was spaghetti slurping. One of my sisters would take one end of a piece of spaghetti, put in her mouth and inhale it with a loud, disgusting noise that ended with an unnerving pop as the other end snapped in and her lips closed shut. That was, without a doubt, grounds for new real estate.

I can't remember even one night, as a child, that we did not eat together—something that seems to have been lost with today's generation of parents and kids. The routine never changed. We passed around the dishes of food that my mom had placed in the center of the table and filled our plates. When your plate was full you sat quietly and waited impatiently until everyone was done serving themselves. We then folded our hands, bowed our heads and said "Bless us our Lord for these thy gifts…," finished the prayer with the sign of the cross and then began eating.

The rules for dinnertime were clear and unbreakable. Besides "no singing at the dinner table" and "no talking with your mouth full," there was "no fighting at the table," "keep your elbows off the table," "eat properly and speak with proper English," (no slang) and "please" and "thank you," of course. If you had a sudden physical urge calling for a sprint to the bathroom you were required to say, "may I be excused, please?" and then you hit the ground running. There were absolutely no phone calls during dinner. And here's the big one; if you wanted a second helping, that is if there was any, you had better wait to see if Dad wanted that last piece of chicken, lasagna, etc. or else!!

Upon relaying this story, it sounds a little like a military school but that's just the way my parents kept control and some semblance of order. All these rules, although annoying for us at the time, helped us know what was expected of us and united us as a family. Throughout my childhood, I believed my family was perfect, maybe because my mom told us just that.

"Burroughs are perfect," she constantly reminded us. "Everyone else has problems and some dysfunction but Burroughs do not."

So, of course, I believed her. I experienced a bit of a shock and temporary devastation when, one day, I realized that I wasn't perfect after all. Nothing monumental occurred to bring me to this conclusion, just a strong dose of reality. It was somewhat comforting to learn that no one is perfect, but it still took me a while to be at peace with my ordinary imperfection. Coming from a tough, abusive childhood herself, I guess my mom just wanted us to feel loved and special. We all certainly did and she still makes us feel that way today!

That modest, simple dining room in our very large house was a gathering place for all of us, not just at dinnertime but all day long. At any one time, there were at least a few of us sitting, talking, playing board games and card games, or doing homework. As we got older, we started going out on dates or with friends until the wee hours. We would all come home around the same time, grab a bag of Doritos, a package of peanut M&M's or maybe a PBJ (peanut butter and jelly) on toast, and head to the dining room. We would while away the early morning hours together talking about our newest love or a recent breakup, friends, experiences, parties, or simply just laughing and joking or acting silly, easily creating genuine, cherished and lasting memories. Today we still come together, although not as often since many of us live in different states. We enjoy the same unity and appreciate with joy and nostalgia the bond that we crafted and continuously experienced in that very special room, at that very special table all those many years ago.

> "CHERISHED FAMILY MEMORIES
> ARE NOT POSSIBLE
> UNLESS THE FAMILY ACTUALLY
> GATHERS TOGETHER
> TO CREATE THEM.
> COMING TOGETHER
> FOR FAMILY DINNERS
> OR SIMPLY TO SHARE WHAT'S
> HAPPENING IN OUR LIVES,
> CAN CREATE AN UNBREAKABLE
> BOND. IT'S NEVER TOO LATE."

# One Plus Seven Equals Eight

"*I*t's time to go everyone. Pack up your stuff and get into the cars," Mom urged. "It's getting late. Kelly, lock up the cabana and be sure to put away the beach chairs and all of you make sure you hang up your bathing suits so that they dry overnight. You have swim team practice first thing in the morning. Don't leave any food here or it will spoil. Put everything in the coolers and bring it home."

We were all tired from the long hours at the beach club but we knew that if we didn't stay organized at the end of the day, the following morning would be chaos. So, we all did our little chores and then, one by one filed into my parents' two cars.

*Bayside Beach and Cabana Club was on the South Shore of Long Island in a town called Freshwaters. It was located right on the beautiful Great South Bay. I still have a hard time fathoming how my parents afforded a membership there. After all, just supporting eight kids pretty much devoured my dad's entire salary. Money was always tight, but somehow they found a way and honestly, I don't really care how, I am just grateful that they did.*

*Memories of my childhood are very sketchy, but the time I spent at Bayside was more about my feelings and emotions as a thirteen- and fourteen-year-old girl who, by the way, was a bit boy crazy at the time. So just thinking about Bayside seems to transport me immediately back to that time and place. We spent every day there, rain or shine. In the middle of the club there were two pools, a game room and a concession area. There was also a large function room where dances were held at night for the teen-aged kids, which happily, fueled my boy obsession. I was particularly attracted to the blond, long-haired surfer type. However, one summer, when I was thirteen, I had three boyfriends (at least I thought so): Tommy, a tennis player, Danny who was a surfer/swimmer and had a boat he made himself called a hydroplane, and then there was Doug. His family was pretty wealthy, I was told, and he had a really cool boat, as well, called a Boston Whaler. On any given day I was pretty certain that at least one of them would be at the club but when they were all there, I was in trouble. In the end, though, it was Danny who stole my heart and was my first real boyfriend.*

*On either side of the beach club were rows of bright red cabanas neatly constructed on "South Shore sand" which I have come to realize is a lot less rocky than the North Shore of Long Island. It wasn't easy to obtain a cabana because there just weren't enough to go around, but my parents had a lot of friends who had been members for a long time, so we were lucky enough to acquire one. Having a cabana made life a lot easier. We had a home base so we didn't have to lug everything back and forth each day. We could leave a lot of our supplies there like towels, bathing suits, clothes, dishes, charcoal, first aid kit, etc.*

*We got to the club as soon as it opened in the morning and stayed until it closed, having all three meals at our home away from home. We had a barbeque grill at the cabana, so we ate a lot of hot dogs and hamburgers during the summer, and sometimes even cooked eggs and bacon for breakfast. Life was carefree and filled with adventure. We kids spent the day swimming, boating, playing pinball, listening to music on the juke box and, for me, falling hopelessly in love with love. There was very little parental supervision because everyone knew everyone and all the adults looked out for each other's children. Mom would bring us there bright and early for swim team practice and Dad would come and meet us after work. At night the kids would gather in the game room or, more to my liking, find a secluded spot to explore one's first attempts at kissing and cuddling. Mom and Dad socialized with their friends, sipping cocktails while sitting in beach chairs by the cabanas until long into the evening.*

So this night was like every other one. Mom and Dad chauffeured us home, a ten or fifteen minute drive, with most of us being so exhausted that we fell asleep on the way. We stumbled into the house and headed off to our respective bedrooms, collapsing into a deep slumber with visions of our day's exciting escapades decorating our dreams.

Morning came quickly and like clockwork Mom called for us to get moving so we wouldn't be late for swim team practice. We all raced around packing our beach bags and Mom loaded up the coolers with the day's nourishment.

"Hurry up guys. Let's go … into the car. Practice starts in fifteen minutes."

Charging down the stairs and out the door we all crammed into Mom's car.

"Where's Charlie," Mom asked anxiously. Did anyone make sure he got up? Sara, go check his room and see if he's still sleeping."

"Uh, Mom, I hate to tell you this," Sara informed us incredulously, a few minutes later. "Charlie is not in his room and he is not in the house. I looked everywhere. His bed has not been slept in. I think we left him."

"What do you mean left him, left him where?"

Suddenly Mom's eyes widened as the absolutely horrifying reality set in that she had actually left her eight-year-old son behind the night before at the beach club. Trying not to panic, we headed frantically to the club. I'm sure my mom's heart was racing as she envisioned every awful thing that might have or could have happened to her little boy as he tried to survive a whole night all alone without his family. We checked the cabana, no Charlie. Mom was visibly shaken by now and the rest of us began showing signs of panic and fear. We then checked the game room— nothing! We ran up and down the beach, even scouring the water's surface as terrifying thoughts tortured our minds. Thank God, we found nothing there! The pool area was still empty from the night before. The only place left to look was the tennis house. "What if he wasn't there, then what? Had we lost him forever?" We opened the doors and entered the common room, scanning the perimeter, hoping and praying we would see him.

"Mom, Mom, look, over there on the couch! He's here, he's here," shrieked Kelly as she went tearing off in the direction of the lounge area.

Sure enough, there he was, curled up in a ball and fast asleep on one of the couches. He had found his way to the tennis house, knowing that there would be a comfortable place for him to sleep.

"Charlie, are you OK?" Mom frantically and tearfully asked gathering him up in her arms and waking him from a deep, peaceful sleep.

Rubbing his eyes, he looked up at all of us and simply said, "I'm fine. I knew you'd come back when you figured it out. It was kind of neat sleeping here."

*So there you have it! Growing up a Burrough was, indeed, filled with adventure, sometimes hinging on a little unintentional child neglect and always bordering on craziness and chaos. However, there was also a perfect faith that the love in our family would help get us through almost anything, even a night of complete and utter abandonment. Bayside provided us all with great fun, lots of laughter and precious memories. Some reminiscences are sentimental and romantic. Others are hilarious, harrowing, and for Mom and Dad, this one particular time, a bit embarrassing as well ... but oh, what a story!*

"IT WAS A CONSTANT STRUGGLE
AND NEARLY IMPOSSIBLE
TO GET THE INDIVIDUAL ATTENTION
THAT WE ALL CRAVED.
HOWEVER,
ONE THING WAS CONSTANT AND
NEVER QUESTIONED OR DOUBTED;
THAT WE WERE ALL LOVED
EQUALLY AND COMPLETELY.
WHAT AN AMAZING GIFT!"

# Silent Memories

"Mom, I'm not wearing this outfit for Easter. I look like an old lady," I announced, throwing my clothes on Mom's bed in a heap. "That disgusting red hat looks like a straw bowl with a bow on it and the grey cape makes me look like a tent … and then there's those pointed, red patent leather shoes, yuk! They look like something a grandmother would wear and do I have to wear those stupid white gloves? I'm getting too old for them. I am twelve years old after all. You might as well stick a sign on my forehead labeling me a geek!"

"Oh Dru, you will look just beautiful," Mom gushed. "I'm sure everyone will love your outfit. Just wait, on Easter morning you will all look like a picture postcard."

I knew there was no talking her out of it but I had to try. Easter was Mom's day to create a fashion show that would turn heads as each of her eight children paraded into church on Easter morning. For as long as I can remember, on the night before Easter, my mom would line up all of our shoes that were polished and shined so that you could see your reflection. My sisters and I all wore bonnets to match our outfits with crisp, clean white gloves to finish the ensemble. My brothers were also dressed to look smart and dapper and sometimes, even had to wear knickers with suspenders, red oxfords and a little Irish cap to boot. It was all a little too much, and as we got older it became harder and harder to endure much less get excited about the mandatory grand entrance and procession down the aisle and into our respective pew. However, Mom was so proud of her brood and my dad backed her up with his firm hand and stern countenance, so we didn't dare protest too much.

Storming off to my room, I glanced at the clock. "Uh oh, it's 11:45," I realized suddenly. "I only have fifteen minutes before the 12:00 noon whistle. I had better eat lunch quick or I'll have to wait until 3:00 p.m."

I made an abrupt about-face and headed toward the kitchen. The rest of my brothers and sisters were already wolfing down peanut butter and jelly sandwiches and a glass of milk and talking about anything and everything, just so they could get it out of their system before that darn whistle blew. I grabbed the bread and slapped a blob of peanut butter on one piece and covered the other with some grape jelly and proceeded to eat as quickly as I could, all the while keeping an eye on the minute hand that was edging closer and closer to 12:00 noon.

It was Good Friday, a very holy day in the Catholic religion and a very sad day as well. My family took every religious holiday seriously, but Good Friday seemed to be a bit more important than the rest. I'm not sure exactly why. Maybe it was because we had to spend so much time thinking about what happened on that horrible, sad day a long time ago. I'm sure everyone knows that Jesus died on the cross on Good Friday and from what I was told He hung there for three long hours, between twelve and three o'clock in the afternoon before he was taken down and buried in a tomb nearby. Sometimes my dad would take time off from work and take us to church so that we could hear the entire story of "The Passion of Christ" as it was read from the Bible scriptures. It was so boring and went on and on for what seemed like hours. After it was over, we would move around the perimeter of the church gazing up at the twelve Stations of the Cross which were statues on the wall that told the story of how Jesus was crucified. I prayed at each station and, even though at twelve years old I felt much removed from the horrific tale, I summoned up some tears in an attempt to prove to myself that I really did understand how awful the crucifixion was and to express my deepest gratitude for the fact that "Jesus died for our sins."

Dad was working on this particular Good Friday, so we were on our own to honor this holy day with the reverence and respect it deserved. The whistle blew and, finished or not, everyone stopped what they were doing and didn't say another word. For the next three hours we were not to eat, drink or speak. We could not watch TV or play games or enjoy any kind of recreation. Our only activities were to read the Bible or any other religious book, say the rosary or pray. We all dispersed to our own little nooks and settled in to contemplate all of the terrible things that Jesus had endured. Occasionally someone would try using sign language to communicate but quickly received a scolding glance from someone else in the group, sending a message loud and clear that this was a blatant breach of the rules.

After some time passed my sister, Susan, gathered us all together by carrying a box that we all knew contained "The Stations Of The Cross." (My dad had taken sticks from the outside, stained them so they were shiny and smooth and then made crosses out of them. He then glued cardboard pictures of each of the thirteen stations onto the crosses). Knowing what was to come next and also without any adult persuasion, we proceeded to the backyard. We placed each of the crosses into the earth all around the yard and then began to say the appropriate prayers at each station. We knelt down and bowed our heads and silently said the words that we all knew by heart. When a certain amount of time elapsed, we rose and moved to the next station. We must have looked like a very strange bunch of kids to the neighborhood children who had climbed up into the tallest trees in their backyards to watch this odd ritual that was taking place. We took no notice of them; well at least *I* tried not to, and continued on with our procession.

The three hours slowly passed and at 3:01 Mom met us all in the kitchen. The air of sadness lifted and, we all started talking at once, so glad to have our voices back. Snacks came out and it was time for another ritual, the annual coloring of the eggs. We gathered around our dining room table and spent a couple of hours laughing and making the most beautiful Easter eggs ever. I always loved taking the white crayon and trying to make swirly, squiggly lines on either end of the egg that matched perfectly, which was a challenge since you couldn't see the white crayon on the white egg as you drew. Using the little wire holder I carefully dipped my eggs into the cups of Paas Food Coloring and then waited for them to magically transform into a rainbow of pastel colored orbs.

Good Friday was an unusual mixture of acute sadness and incredible joy. It seems to me that it strangely mirrored life. Just as life on earth does not allow us to escape sadness it also does not deprive us of joy either. We had our sad times and our joyful ones, just as we do today. We had our share of normal sibling rivalry and silly meaningless bickering. However, what we have today, more than anything else, are warm and blessed memories. We remember fondly that our lives were shaped by a message of love that was given to us by our parents and our faith and one that we embrace and cherish immensely. We were, and still are a strong family, we Burroughs, united by our faith and committed to each other in every way. So as Good Friday arrives as it always does, I spend a moment to honor all of those wonderful memories. I contemplate what this special Christian holiday means and how it shaped and strengthened our beautiful family.

"MY FAMILY TRADITIONS ARE
RICH AND COHESIVE ELEMENTS OF
MY CHILDHOOD. THEY ALLOW ME
TO FEEL AN INDIVIDUAL SENSE OF
CONNECTEDNESS TO A GREATER
WHOLE, JUST AS LIVING AS A
HUMAN BEING CONNECTS ME
TO ALL OF HUMANITY."

# *"Go Team Go"*

*A*s the sales conference was coming to a close its facilitator, Henry, asked us all to do one final exercise. "Think of a time in your life when you felt successful. Remember what that felt like. Visualize the experience in every detail." I closed my eyes and slowly drifted back in time scanning various ages trying to pull up the experience that evoked absolute triumph and total success.

*I found myself at the age of fourteen about ready to enter the ninth grade. I spent grades one through eight in Catholic school, and I was so excited to be starting my high school years in public school. No more nuns, with in my opinion, overly strict rules, who were completely out of touch with teenagers. I don't think one of them was under seventy years of age. No more stuffy uniforms that had to be worn below the knee. It was the late '60s after all—the era of the mini skirt! No more eating lunch in our classroom, or having a playground that also functioned as the church parking lot. I was now looking forward to actually having boys in my class, studying subjects like art and music, and most importantly, having gym class. I had been taking dance and gymnastics with a private teacher for years. Gymnastics was what I loved more than anything and every day of that last year in Catholic school, I dreamed of trying out for the cheerleading squad in junior high school.*

Pulled, for a moment, out of my past regression experience, I wondered why I had wanted this so badly. Was it because throughout my childhood I felt so invisible being one of eight children and I needed to be noticed? Was it because my father had insisted that we were all swimmers and divers and I wanted to rebel and find my own way? That was it! I knew that if I could just find a different "label" other than swimmer or diver or even "Burrough," I would be special and unique. Then I could finally begin to define who Drusilla was. I wanted an identity so badly and I decided that no one was going to stop me. Of course, back then I don't think I really understood any of this, only that I had to make the cheerleading squad no matter what!

*After the first day of school there was practice in the gym. I was so excited but extremely nervous. I didn't know anyone and believe it or not, I was very shy. As I entered the gym I noticed groups of girls gathered together practicing the cheers. There had to be a hundred. I wandered around at first not sure what to do. All the groups seemed to be predetermined and, I, of course, was on the outside looking in. As I watched, it was clear that everyone knew all the cheers. I didn't know any. There was one group all the other girls were watching and trying to emulate, and from a few conversations I overheard, it became clear that they were the ones to beat. As I searched for a place to fit in, I felt lost, alone and again, completely invisible.*

*"Why are you doing this? What makes you think you will be chosen? Look at all these girls. They've been practicing for two years. No one even knows who you are. Maybe you should slip out quietly and forget the whole thing. You know how afraid you are to perform in front of people or to be judged. You realize it will be only* you *out there all by yourself when you do that silly cheer you made up. Get out of here now before you make a fool of yourself."*

*"Not a chance," I shot back at my frightened, insecure self. "I dreamed about this for too long. I can do it even if I am scared. I'm good ... just as good as anyone here if not better."*

*I pushed any negative thoughts out of my head determined to follow my dream. After walking up to several groups who looked at me and then turned away making me believe that I was not welcome, I found a group that reluctantly allowed me to practice with them. During the three days of practice no one took much notice of me and I was pretty quiet as I practiced the cheers and worked tirelessly on the one I was required to make up myself.*

*"Try out" day arrived! At first we came out in groups and did a "group cheer" and the panel of teachers sitting on the bleachers judged us, then secretly recorded their scores. Next we were rated on our individual cheer that we created. It was finally my turn. I walked slowly to the center of the gym. I heard everyone begin whispering and asking each other who I was. Of course, perhaps it was my self-consciousness that assumed this. My stomach was so tied up in knots that I felt nauseous and my heart was about to do a pole vault right out of my chest. I could feel the blood pool in my cheeks and my neck, my whole body was trembling and I felt faint.*

*"How in the world was I going to do this?"*

*I stood in front of the judges and began. Suddenly and without warning something incredible happened to that shy, quiet young girl. She came alive and transformed into a self-assured and outgoing competitor. A deep, loud, crisp voice burst forth traveling to all corners of the huge gym surprising even me. My body seemed to move like a champion showcasing my gymnastic ability with what felt like flawless precision. In only a few short minutes I slapped my hands down to the sides of my thighs in a dramatic finish. For a moment no one said anything. The judges looked back and forth at each other and there was a strange eerie silence. I wasn't sure what to do but finally the judges thanked me and I walked off the floor and sat down.*

*"OK, I did great. Did I do great? Yes, I did. At least I did my best*

*but was it good enough? It had to be. It just had to be," I demanded des-*
*perately as I closed my eyes and said a quick prayer hoping that would*
*seal the deal.*

*Try outs ended and we were told that the eight girls chosen for the*
*squad would be posted the following morning on the doors of the gym.*
*The next morning I got to the school early. As I walked down the endless*
*halls to the gym I couldn't feel my body. I felt as if I was outside of it just*
*observing. I think the emotion going on inside of me was too much so I just*
*vacated it for the moment. The intensity of my dream was so overwhelming*
*you'd have thought it was a matter of life and death.*

*The doors of the gym loomed large in front of me. I kept my eyes*
*shut tight as tears welled up beneath my closed lids. After a few moments*
*I opened them and began to scan the list. There it was! I blinked hard and*
*looked again, Drusilla Burrough!*

*"I made it. I really made it! Does this mean I'm not invisible anymore?*
*Will people finally see me?"*

*All around me some girls were crying and others were cheering.*
*People were congratulating me and asking me who I was and where I*
*came from. I felt triumphant! I was finally somebody! I was special! I was*
*now more than one spoke in a wheel! I mattered! Dru mattered! I did this*
*all by myself without any help from anyone just me! Wow, what a feeling!*

"Time's up," called Henry from the conference podium. "We have
to wrap things up pretty soon." I opened my eyes. I fought back tears but
decided to just let them flow as I felt a liberating release and reveled in a
long forgotten memory. I wrapped my arms around myself as if to embrace
that shy, determined, courageous child that was me. My journey to 1968
seemed so real. It was amazing to actually be that young girl again. It
wasn't just a memory. I was there. I re-experienced all the emotions and

feelings as if they were happening that day. I felt a little foolish having fixated on such a seemingly insignificant moment but for that fourteen-year-old Dru, it was huge. It was a tender, scary, triumphant memory, and I knew immediately why it was my greatest success. I faced my fears. I moved out of my comfort zone and reached for my dream and I succeeded. I realize now that this one achievement did not define me, of course, but it was the beginning. It was the start of a discovery process that would help me to know Dru, the physical human being fully grounded in the earth plane, and Dru, the being of eternal, divine light—my soul. The experience represented, for me, unity and individuality. I was part of a unit, my family, and yet I was a unique and special person who would do wonderful and gratifying work in the world that only I could do. I needed both! On the grander scale I was part of the whole of humanity, a necessary cell for the successful functioning of the entire global human body!

Of course then, at that moment, I didn't care at all about any of that. All I knew was that I kicked butt! I was the best of the best! I was a cheerleader! Whooohooo!

"DUALITY IS AN ILLUSION!
WE ARE ALL CONNECTED BY THE
SAME DIVINE UNIFYING FORCE.
YET, OUR UNIQUE CONTRIBUTION
IS ESSENTIAL IN ORDER TO
GENERATE HEALTH AND CONTINUED
GROWTH FOR THE WHOLE!
OUR FULLEST POTENTIAL
USUALLY LIES JUST OUTSIDE
OUR COMFORT ZONE."

# Dormant Memories

He wasn't really our uncle. Mom and Dad, both being only children, didn't provide us with any genuine aunts or uncles. He was my dad's cousin. To all eight of us, however, he was Uncle Archie or "Unc" as we affectionately called him. He was the only extended family we had. My dad's father died when he was only twelve and his mom died when I was five years old. Both of my mom's parents were alive and lived fairly close by. However, they were heavy drinkers and neither of my parents drank much, so we rarely had alcohol in the house. I don't think my grandparents thought it was much fun visiting us, and they hardly ever did.

Unc lived in a small apartment in Queens, NY. He was single, never married, and had no children of his own. I don't know what he did for work but whatever it was; he had his weekends free and almost every weekend during my childhood he came to stay with us. Fridays were always so exciting, as we waited for him to arrive. He drove a small white sports car that I thought was ultra cool since, when we were very young, we only had a big, ugly, black Desoto. I remember he wore a brown fedora with a little red feather that I thought was sophisticated.

Finally, someone would call out "Unc's here," and we all bolted out the door to greet him. His car was the equivalent of a fully packed Santa's sleigh on Christmas Eve. The trunk was always brimming with toys. I don't think he predetermined who each toy was for, only that there was enough to go around and we scrambled to see who would get the "primo" gift. Somehow, though, it didn't matter. We were all so happy with whatever we got. We didn't have a lot of money, so gifts were mainly given on birthdays, Christmas, and of course, when Unc rode into town.

His glove compartment had an abundant supply of Wrigley's fruit stripe gum. We each got a pack and I can often remember putting the whole thing in my mouth at once, much to my mom's dismay as she repeatedly told me that chewing gum, especially that much at once, wasn't very ladylike.

This routine went on for many years as we celebrated everyday life, special occasions and holidays with Mom, Dad, all eight kids, and Unc. The only thing that bothered me during that time was that my brothers and sisters always said that I was Unc's favorite. I hated it! I was always labeled as looking different and my siblings would tease me and say I was adopted. In those early years, until I was about twelve, I just wanted to be like everyone else in the family. After all, we were "Burroughs"— special, proud and perfect in every way, as Mom frequently told us. So if I was different, then I wasn't any of those things. This was really painful to me and I remember, many times, flying up the stairs to my room in tears believing that I wasn't as wonderful and "perfect" as everyone else.

So, my childhood turned to adolescence. Then I moved to my teenage years and on to my emergence as a young woman. At twenty-one I didn't think much about Unc. He had eventually met a woman named Lucy who was twenty years younger than him and at age "fifty-something," he married and finally became a father of a young boy named Roger. We didn't see him much at all after that. Truthfully, during my teen years, his visits became less frequent. I figured we weren't much fun anymore since we were no longer kids and we had begun living our own lives. All and all, though, my memories of Unc were good ones until....

I was in my early twenties waitressing at a local restaurant. One night it was unusually slow and I only had one table, a young couple sitting at an intimate spot by the window. They seemed to be very much in love as they held hands, talked softly and occasionally shared a tender kiss. The man was so affectionate and I was thinking how nice it would be to be treated that way. He removed his hand from hers and softly laid it on her back and began gently rubbing it in a circular motion. As he continued I became more and more agitated.

"This is weird," I thought to myself anxiously. "Why in the world would this bother me?"

It did and as he continued I started screaming in my head, "Stop it, stop it!" Without warning, a memory flashed in my mind of my Uncle Archie with his hand under my shirt, rubbing my back in a very sensual way. I seemed to be about ten years old. I remember feeling like I wanted to scream and wanting to tell him to stop. Yet, I was taught by my parents to respect adults and not to be rude. So I let it continue and pretended that it was OK, at the same time praying to God to make this awful moment end. Instantaneously, I moved to another memory. I was lying on my parent's bed and my uncle was on top of me. Thankfully, he was clothed but I remember saying, "Uncle Archie, there's something in your pocket and it's hurting me." I said it over and over. He was heavy and I couldn't move. He ignored my pleas to remove the object that was causing me pain. He continued to move his body around and around over mine and there was nothing I could do about it.

Suddenly, I was jolted back to the present!

"Oh my God," I shrieked in my mind. "Could this be true? Did this really happen? Was there more that I still didn't remember? Why hadn't I remembered this until now?"

I had no answers but was determined to find them. I went home to my parent's house and confronted my mom.

"I remembered something, Mom. It was an awful memory. It was about Uncle Archie."

The look on her face told me that she knew exactly what I was about to tell her and that it was, in fact, true. I continued to describe in detail the horrible memories and then waited for her response.

"Yes, Dru, it did happen. It happened when you were ten years old. You never said a word about it to me. The only way I found out was because of Kelly (my older sister). He tried to do something to her but Kelly stopped him and then came to Dad and me and told us what had happened. Later, when we talked to you, we found out what he had done to you."

I sat there stunned. I didn't cry. I wasn't angry. I was just shocked and trying to comprehend everything. Not only was it impossible to believe, but I also couldn't understand why I had suppressed the memory for so long. I guess it must have been very traumatic for me.

"Did you take us to counseling or get us any help at all?"

"No," Mom said with complete confidence. "I just figured that if we made a big deal about it, it would become a big deal. If we just forgot about it, everything would be fine and our family would be the same as it had always been. Dad talked to him and made it clear that Unc would never ever touch any of you again. After that," she continued, "he stopped coming around as much and eventually stopped coming at all."

I left there that day feeling betrayed. How could he have done this to a little girl, especially a little girl who loved and trusted him? I began to understand why I had so much trouble setting boundaries, and also when I did, why I could never protect them and prevent people from overstepping them. Maybe, this was one of the reasons why it was so hard for me to say "NO" when I really wanted to. Retrieving that memory was painful, but it helped me to find some of the missing pieces of my life that caused me to behave in ways that were not healthy. I got some counseling so that I could process the whole experience better. I can honestly say I have never felt anger toward my uncle, just pity, disgust and terrible disappointment.

Over the years I learned to love myself better. While my nature is to want to help others and to be of service in the world, I have learned that if I don't put myself first, respect my own boundaries and say "no" when I do not want or I'm unable to do something for whatever reason, I am not honoring myself—body, mind or spirit. I now choose to nurture myself first so that I can be strong, healthy and able to serve those in need of the gifts of love, compassion and healing that I am capable of giving.

"I MUST ALWAYS ESTABLISH AND
ENFORCE REASONABLE BOUNDARIES
IN ORDER TO NURTURE
AND PROTECT MYSELF.
WHETHER ONE IS AN ADULT
OR A CHILD,
IF SOMETHING SOMEONE IS DOING
DOESN'T FEEL COMFORTABLE,
WE HAVE EVERY RIGHT TO SAY
STOP!"

# Pondering My Purpose

It wasn't so very long ago
That she entered this mysterious world.
As a child she always wondered,
"Who is this little girl?"

Why did she come to this Earth?
What is her purpose in life?
Would she find her answers in flowers that grow
Or a full moon on a bright starry night?

When she grew to be a woman,
A voice inside her said,
"Seek the answers from your parents—
What they did, how they lived, what they said."

She journeyed to her childhood.
She felt happy, joyful and safe.
As she traveled farther back in time,
She found answers in that sacred place.

She saw her parents overcome adversity
From childhoods filled with pain.
She discovered that despite their confusion and loss,
They were determined it wouldn't be in vain.

They reached to the heavens for their answers;
They embraced their faith in the Lord.
He provided a steady vessel
When they were uncertain they could reach the other shore.

Her answers, she found in their hope,
And in God, the way to the truth.
She learned though life could be painful,
There's wisdom in both the old age and youth.

So this poem is her way to say thank you
For their love and the lives that they shared.
She remembered her soul because of their love;
She is strong because they both cared.

"MY PARENTS WERE
ONCE CHILDREN,
THOUGH AT TIMES IT IS
HARD TO IMAGINE.
LEARNING ABOUT THEIR HISTORY
AND REMEMBERING MY OWN
HELPED ME TO DISCOVER WHO
I AM AND HAVE ALWAYS BEEN."

# Breaking Away

# Introduction to Breaking Away

So now you have an idea of what it was like growing up in my home. Hearing those stories will make it easy, or at times really hard, to understand why I saw myself and my life the way I did and why I made the choices I did as a young adult. Fortunately, I make it a bit simpler for you. Of all the times in my life so far, this was the most confusing, painful, and agonizing. For these reasons, I spent much, much time in meditation, prayer and counseling in order to understand young Drusilla. Why had she become so damaged when, from the outside looking in, her life seemed so wonderful? Why was she so different from her five sisters and two brothers? Was she really that different or was it just her unique perception?

I believe we are eternal souls coming to earth lifetime after lifetime with memory imprints buried deep in our subconscious and carried forward from those other lives. Sometimes, because of past life experiences, we have irrational phobias or fears that have their roots in those times long ago. For example, perhaps we drowned in a previous life and now have a terrible fear of the water. It isn't necessary to know about our past lives, only that some of the unexplained parts of our personalities can be understood with this awareness. I believe this allows us to be gentler with ourselves when we attempt to let go and heal from things we may not fully understand.

I also believe we choose our parents and our unique circumstances in order for us to fulfill our life purpose and to learn our lessons. I believe we have pre-birth planning sessions with our guides where we create our sacred contracts with other souls. These other souls agree to play a particular role in our lives so that we can accomplish our goals and remember our soul's light. Even those who torture and torment us may have chosen to do so out of love so that we can grow by experiencing contrast. For example, being abused and feeling powerless as a child may force us to go within and remember the power and strength of our divine self. This I believe was in part, the reason for my relationship with my first husband Jake. It was a difficult, tumultuous relationship. However, as I say over and over throughout this book, "our greatest adversaries are our greatest teachers."

Jake was an amazing teacher for me. The most peaceful place for me to have gone to, in order to endure that time period, was deep within where the truth about who I am and who I have always been was revealed to me. I believe it was necessary for me to feel worthless and filled with self-doubt, so I could experience the contrast—remembering that I am a magnificent, powerful and divinely beautiful soul. Though I can honestly say that I am grateful for everything I learned from our dysfunctional relationship, I now understand that as a human being with free will, I could have learned the same lessons in a more gentle way by making different choices. Jake could have made different choices, as well. Perhaps, there was a woman more suited to him and one that would have made him feel more content. Yet, we made the choices we did and shame, blame and regret serve no useful purpose in the growth and remembrance of the soul's light. The lessons that we come here to learn do not change, for the most part, but there are always different possible choices we and other souls can make in order to help each other accomplish our life plan.

As you continue to read, I hope you and I are becoming closer in spirit and that you see me as a fellow traveler and a loyal, supportive friend who you have yet to meet in person. Perhaps, someday we will. As with each past section, remember to focus on the feelings and emotions as well as the lessons, insights and wisdom that I share with you. What experiences in your own life come to mind as you read about mine? Think about the key people throughout your life who have taught valuable lessons, both the loving ones and the not so loving ones. Whatever surfaces for you is exactly what your guides and your angels are trying to help you work with, so that you can better understand yourself, your friends and family, and your life purpose. These insights are ultimately what will help you become fully grounded on your predestined path and what will bring you the kind of peace and love that we are all seeking.

Let your pen or your keys come alive! Write your story and discover your wisdom. I can't wait to hear about it!

# *Jake and Me*

"So now what," I wondered, feeling paralyzing waves of intense anxiety wash over me.

Suddenly I was eighteen years old. My two older sisters went off to college. I was a senior in high school and didn't have any idea who I was, who I wanted to become, or what I wanted to do with my life. How could that be? To an outsider looking in, I seemed to have it all. I was attractive. I was popular. I was a cheerleader, a member of the gymnastics team, president of the French Club, and I had a boyfriend who was popular and athletic. All of this should have resulted in a fully grounded, well-adjusted, young adult who had a good sense of self and good self-esteem … not by a long shot!

As you know, both of my parents had no siblings. They didn't know what it was like to have brothers and sisters themselves; so of course, they didn't know how to raise eight children. Therefore, they did the only thing that made sense to them. They raised us as a unit—Company "B." Dad was the commanding officer and he did not encourage any challenge to his authority. He made the rules. They were "Burrough" rules and we all had "Burrough" morals and values. Any attempt to rise up and speak one's mind was quickly crushed, and we learned to just "stay in line," think like a Burrough, and behave like a Burrough; at least I did anyway. There was strength in numbers. Our number was eight … eight children, and my number was three—the third born. I was one spoke in a wheel. Together we moved forward. Together I felt safe and I had an identity even though, at the same time, I was desperately longing for my own individuality. The town in which we lived in was not that large but our family was. We had a good reputation and were a respected family. All I needed to do was to say I was a Burrough, and it was "a given" that I was a good kid. Being attractive seemed to be the only thing that made me stand out on my own. My looks made me special, or so I thought. The only time I remember getting any individual attention from my dad was when I overheard him say, "I'm worried about her; she's too pretty." This was hardly a very substantial compliment, but it was something, and I went with it. I started to identify with my physical form. How I looked became who I was. I started to realize that I could get what I wanted just because of how I looked. The problem was I didn't really know what I wanted, because I didn't know who I was. This unhealthy focus led me to make some pretty destructive choices in my early adulthood.

Obviously, I couldn't stay a child and live at home forever. I had to grow up, like it or not. Getting out on my own was the next logical step. I was terrified. I believed that Drusilla, all by herself, was nothing. She had no mind of her own. She had a Burrough mind. I had been rather sheltered as well, believing that all people were basically good and my upbringing, with all of its emphasis on faith and religion, made me naïve to the danger and chaos that existed in the world.

As frightened as I was to venture out into the world, I had pride as well; if my two older sisters could do it, then so could I. I applied to college and off I went. It was a scary place for me. I missed home. I was lonely and the drug culture of the early seventies was something that I was not even slightly prepared for. I felt like I was in a foreign country and couldn't speak the language. Then I met Jake. I was on the gymnastics team and he was on the wrestling team. We started dating and I ended the relationship with my hometown boyfriend. It seemed like Jake was everything I was not. I saw him as my "shadow side" that I was never able to express. I followed the rules, respected authority, and never challenged it. He seemed like a rebel, challenging and questioning authority at every turn. He loved living on the edge and "flying by the seat of his pants." I was fascinated and became caught up in his wild, fun life, and at the same time, tried to hold fast to the image of "good Catholic girl." I thought that the internal label of being Catholic, as well as being a pretty girl, were the only identities I had. Before college, I relied on my family to provide me with a good moral compass. Suddenly, they weren't there. It was just me. I felt incomplete and I was desperate to find that completeness. I decided the only way to do that was to be in a relationship. I chose Jake.

Though I didn't understand at the time, I have since learned that we attract people into our lives based upon our opinions and perceptions about ourselves. Whatever we think about in the privacy of our own mind creates our life. We draw into our lives, people and circumstances that support how we think about ourselves and the world. I was insecure and felt unworthy. Jake was young, eighteen years old, and had on his mind what most boys his age did. He loved pretty girls. Although, I'm sure there was more to him at the time, it seemed to me, that my looks were the only thing that was important. Since, I also believed that the only redeeming quality about me was my outer appearance, I was a perfect fit. I often felt I was just a toy for him, to be played with and then tossed away when something better, a more exciting escapade, caught his attention. Yet, I stayed anyway hoping things would get better and I would rise higher on his list of priorities. I don't think I ever did. I was unable to see that this was a recipe for disaster, and I was completely unaware that I was setting myself up for a long and complicated relationship, and a lot of pain and heartache. I jumped in headfirst and then couldn't seem to find my way back to the shore for a very long time.

For a while it was all very exciting. I was whisked into a world filled with partying and wild adventures. However, over the years I longed for something more meaningful. I wanted to feel loved and cherished but by then I was stuck and unhappy in the relationship. I was afraid to leave because being alone terrified me. So I pushed aside my dreams, married Jake and began living vicariously through him in a very unhealthy way. I was slowly losing myself more and more every day. Jake didn't change. He was the same Jake I met when I was in college but I began to change. Perhaps, I was beginning to have sparks of remembrance about who my real authentic self was, and I wanted her back. Jake didn't understand why I was so unhappy and that made him angry. So, I tried desperately to make our marriage work, ignoring the still small voice inside of me. Eventually my soul sank deeper and deeper within me until I no longer remembered who I was at all, what I loved as a child, or what had given me joy. I felt as if I had died while I was still alive.

Before I married Jake, in November of 1980, I remember that two days before the wedding my mom took me into her bedroom, sat me down on the bed and began to cry.

"Please, Dru, don't marry Jake. I know if you do, you will be making the biggest mistake of your life. I just don't think he is the right one for you."

Somewhere inside, I knew she was right but it was too late. I couldn't turn back then. The sad thing about our relationship was that I never felt that Jake didn't love me. He just couldn't love me the way I needed to be loved. He seemed angry all the time, and the anger scared me more and more. I also felt like he wanted to be anywhere else but at home with me. So many nights I waited hours for him to come home after he said he'd only be gone for an hour. When he finally did I could tell he'd been drinking. I couldn't talk to him so I just quietly and mournfully slipped into bed to avoid any confrontation. Despite his behavior, I believed Jake wanted to be loved and to love me, but his kind of love didn't make me feel cherished. I felt hurt and abandoned. I don't think he liked being married too much and wanted his freedom, but at the same time he wanted me too. It was confusing.

I endured the sixteen years of our union by living a lie. I created a fantasy world in my mind. During the day, when he was gone, I pretended and believed that things were not as bad as they actually were. I wrote poems to him and letters, and I professed my love. I bought tapes on relationships and read books about how to communicate better, and I lived my days in a bubble of hope and optimism. That bubble quickly became an ethereal mist that gathered in my eyes and streamed down my cheeks each night that he came home. My fairy tale became a sad reality when I realized, once again, that what we had was not the love I wanted. So I cried myself to sleep at night and woke up in the morning with self-induced amnesia and a commitment to continue living my lie.

As part of my detachment from reality, I continued living in the future. The pain of the present was unbearable, so I started living in "someday." It started with, "when we get married, things will be better and my life will begin." Then, "when we have children, he will become more mature and things will be better and our good life together will begin." We did have three children—one boy and two girls. Things only got worse as our responsibilities mounted. Eventually, when the pain of the present became far greater than the fear of the unknown and the dread of being alone, my "someday" became, "when I get divorced, my joy will finally return and my life will begin." That, and an intense, ever-growing quest for *spiritual* truth, was what it took for me to finally make the decision to file for divorce. I thought that was the hardest decision I would ever make in my life and the greatest challenge I would ever face. It was only the beginning, however, as an adversarial child custody case ensued. A difficult, unstoppable descent into an abyss of darkness, sadness, and fear challenged my soul and my spirit. There was no escape from it, no alternate route. I had to go through it. It was a trial by fire and it burned deep and lasting scars into every corner of my weeping heart. My dream of a perfect marriage with Jake and a united happy family was coming to an end, and the sadness was overwhelming. It took all the strength I had and all I didn't know existed in order to survive. I did manage to survive, but the fallout took its toll and caused painful wounds that have thankfully scarred over with time. Yet, they are a constant reminder of my firm commitment to choose daily a life of love, peace, and joy.

"OUR GREATEST ADVERSARIES ARE OUR GREATEST TEACHERS. MINE WAS JAKE, AND I SUPPOSE I WAS HIS. UNDERSTANDING MY CHILDHOOD HELPED ME UNDERSTAND MYSELF BETTER AND THE CHOICES I MADE. IT ALL HAPPENED PERFECTLY SO THAT I COULD BECOME THE STRONG, LOVING, PEACEFUL WARRIOR SPIRIT I AM TODAY, WHO IN TURN HELPS OTHERS DO THE SAME."

# *Quest for Fertility*

"Hey, guess you got it, huh? Are you OK?" my husband Jake asked leaning against the door frame, arms crossed in front of his chest as if to protect himself from the waves of anguish and despair that were radiating from my core.

"No, I'm not OK," I sobbed sitting on the bathroom floor in a fetal position, arms wrapped around my legs, my face buried in my knees. I reluctantly lifted my head revealing eyes that were nearly swollen shut and a face streaked with a thousand mournful tears I had shed over the course of the last hour. "I will be, though, I just need to cry a little longer."

"OK," he murmured as he slowly turned and left. He knew by then that there was nothing he could do to comfort me. This moment had become a dreaded ritual that repeated itself like clockwork every twenty-eight days for the last two and a half years. As difficult as my marriage to Jake was, I have a few tender memories of this time when I could tell that he was really hurting for me and truly wished he could take away my pain.

Our lives, or at least mine, had been overcome by endless doctor's appointments for fertility testing and monitoring my temperature for the exact moment of ovulation and trying many different drugs. Those anxious, desperate moments of coming together had lost all spontaneity and passion. And then, of course, there was the constant pleading and praying to God; "Please, please let this be the month that I conceive."

At the beginning of each new cycle, I had renewed hope and faith that this time it would happen. I spent two weeks anticipating and imagining how those two amazing pieces of genetic material would find their way through biological pathways in order to merge together, thus creating our tiny miracle. Then conception day would come. We hoped that "all systems were a go" and we each released the necessary components for a successful outcome. It was no longer a romantic encounter, but a strategically planned and calculated act, devoid of much emotion or joy. I stayed in bed far longer than I needed to, in order to give that tiny tadpole-looking creature enough time to reach its expectant home.

The following two weeks, I obsessed and dreamed about the life I was absolutely certain was growing inside of me. I began looking at "baby stuff" of all kinds. I even started drinking more milk and eating more fruits and vegetables in order to give our child proper nutrition right from the start. I wouldn't allow myself to imagine that we had failed. Inevitably, the fateful day came, once again. The realization that my prayers remained unanswered overwhelmed me, and I dropped to the bathroom floor to mourn something that never was and something I wanted so desperately to be.

It was the summer of 1985. I had just finished working a late shift at a local restaurant. I arrived at my car and noticed a small piece of paper on my windshield. I took it off and got into my car. I turned on the inside light. It was an advertisement for a psychic. I started to crumple it up but something stopped me. I opened it back up and looked at it again.

"Maybe this is a sign from God or something," I thought.

Earlier in the day, I prayed and asked God to please let me know whether I was to have children or not. The anxiety and panic attacks were getting worse and I knew that I might have to accept that being a mother was not part of my path. If I didn't, I was afraid that all of the emotional stress might cause physical illness as well. I figured that this was the answer to my prayer. So I put the paper in my pocketbook and decided to call the next day and make an appointment.

Her name was Kaitlin. I arrived at her house at 2:00 p.m. I stood at the door for a few minutes trying to resolve the inner conflict going on since I now decided to go to my first psychic.

"I really don't think the Catholic Church would approve of this whole thing. Maybe this isn't such a good idea," came a tiny voice from one shoulder.

"And maybe," responded the voice form the opposing side, "the Catholic Church doesn't have all the answers either. Maybe I need to follow my own gut for a change instead of listening to everyone else, including the church. I'm going to do this. I have to."

The door opened and a very large Hispanic woman greeted me. "You must be Drusilla," she said extending her hand. She had a kind face and a gentle smile. She didn't look weird, just like a regular person. I followed her into a small room that was adorned with lots of statues and pictures of Jesus and other religious figures and saints. I felt better and more at ease.

"Psychics could be Christians too," I supposed. "Who knew?"

I told her nothing about me or why I was there. I decided that I would have a tarot card reading for $25.00. I shuffled the cards and she began turning them over one by one. She studied them carefully for a moment and then lifted her head.

"You have been trying to get pregnant for quite some time and have been unsuccessful," she revealed.

I was shocked but didn't let on. I maintained my poker face so as not to give her any help at all. I just listened.

"You will get pregnant in one to three months. You will get pregnant with twins but only one will survive and it will be a boy."

She went on to tell me some other things, but I really don't remember what they were. I got the answer that I wanted and for some strange reason,

I believed her completely.

The next month I was trying a new drug called Pergonal. My husband had to inject me with it each night for ten days up to the day of ovulation. I remember that day so clearly. I took the whole day off from work so I could concentrate on making a baby. I don't know why I thought it would take all day but I was not thinking all that clearly during that time. Afterward, I stayed in bed for the rest of the day. I imagined what was going on, or at least what I hoped was going on inside of me. Following "creation day," I went through my normal two week ritual as the anxiety level rose higher and higher, the closer I got to the end of my cycle. However, the twenty-eight day marker came and went. It was hard to contain my excitement, but I had to. I didn't want to get my hopes up too high. I had been disappointed so many times. If I went too high emotionally, and I wasn't pregnant, the fall would be devastating. I didn't do a home pregnancy test because I wanted to be absolutely sure that the result was correct. I went to the doctor's office in the morning and had a blood test. They told me they would call later and let me know what the test revealed. That day seemed to drag on forever. I sat on the couch for hours clutching my favorite teddy bear, "Grandpa Joe," and just staring at the phone. Finally, it rang. My heart started pounding in my chest and my hands were trembling as I tentatively picked it up.

"Mrs. Mainer, this is Dana Thomas, a nurse in Dr. Shurld's office."

"Yes, this is Mrs. Mainer," I replied, barely audible and still anxiously clutching "Grandpa Joe."

"Congratulations, you're pregnant," she announced joyfully.

"Are you sure?" I pleaded, as warm tears of joy began to fall slowly from my wide eyes. "I mean are you really, really sure?"

She assured me that there was no doubt at all. I was having a baby.

The next four weeks flew by. I was on cloud nine. I didn't know if I was pregnant with twins, but I did know I was definitely pregnant. Then sometime during the sixth week, I started to bleed.

"Oh my God no, this can't be happening. I'm having a miscarriage," I screamed with absolute horror.

I was frantic and terrified, so I did what any rational person in this situation would do. No, I didn't call my doctor. I called my local psychic. I was crying so hard she could barely understand me. When I finished explaining what was going on, she paused for a moment or two.

"Drusilla, you need to calm down," she commanded. "There are two babies. One is fine and the other is not. If you don't stay calm, you will jeopardize the healthy one."

It never occurred to me that her prediction regarding one of my babies not surviving, would be the result of a miscarriage. For some reason I thought one baby would die at birth. I was suddenly very calm and peaceful. I completely believed what she had told me. I hung up the phone and explained to my husband exactly what she said. I guess I should have been sad that one of the fetuses didn't make it, but all I could feel was relief. My husband just shook his head, looking at me as if I had lost my mind and urged me to call the doctor. I did and the next day we went to his office to have a sonogram performed. Once it was completed, the doctor called us both into his office.

"Well, Mr. and Mrs. Mainer, there are two embryonic sacs. One is disintegrating and one is thriving. Unfortunately, you did lose one, but the other should be just fine."

I looked over at my husband, whose lower jaw was nearly scraping the floor. I shot him an "I told you so" look and then just smiled. The doctor ordered me to be on bed rest for the duration of the pregnancy, and seven-and-a-half months later I delivered a healthy, beautiful, perfect baby boy.

"SOME DREAMS ARE SO BIG
THAT NOTHING CAN GET IN THE WAY
OF ACHIEVING THEM.
BEING A MOTHER
WAS MY GREATEST DREAM,
AND MY CHILDREN
ARE MY GREATEST GIFTS."

# The Unborn World

*(Dedicated and inspired by my son, Jake Asher, born 4/6/86)*

Tremors of life stir within my womb
Like the ebb and flow of a restless tide.
It gathers strength from a celestial source.
Who are you?
What have you come to accomplish?
What is your purpose for being?

Beyond the realm of this lifetime
Lie the secrets of unborn life.
Beyond my mortal awareness
Dwell the visions of unborn dreams.

This evolving entity catapults me
To the outer limits of this sacred world,
But a force far greater than my own
Precludes my entrance, therein.

If only I could glimpse the countenance
Of the "Fetal Lord,"
Ask the questions
That swirl anxiously in my heart.

Something prevents my quest.
Unable to penetrate the veil
Leading to that cryptic sphere,
I endlessly continue to probe
The unfathomed infinity of that unborn place;
Continue to de-riddle the hidden mysteries of genesis.

Perhaps the answers lie not so far away,
But right here—within.

"THE SENSATION OF LIFE
GROWING INSIDE OF ME EVOKED
AWE, QUESTIONS, GRATITUDE
AND AN ACCEPTANCE OF AN
UNWORLDLY AND TEMPORARILY
UNSOLVABLE MYSTERY.
FOR ME, IT WAS THE BEGINNING
OF A LIFETIME JOURNEY OF
DISCOVERING SPIRIT AND TRUTH."

# *My Angel in a White Fedora*

"*K*yle and Callie, stay to the right side of the boardwalk," shouted my sister to her seven-year-old son and five-year-old daughter, who were still learning to negotiate their bicycles.

Spring's majesty and brilliance were just beginning to unfold. It was beckoning all of us to emerge from our long winter hibernation into the blooms of daffodils, tulips, and the consistent promise of warming, glorious rays of sunshine, gentle, soft breezes, and an abundance of new life.

"Jake and Brianne, make sure you don't separate from each other, but don't get too close or you'll collide," I instructed my son, also seven, and my daughter, six.

My sister, Marianna and I had decided to take advantage of the incredible, sparkling June day and go to a seaside park. This park is located on the north shore, right on the Long Island Sound. It's unique and diverse landscape includes three miles of sandy beach with glacier-formed bluffs to the west of the shoreline. There are mud flats, a bird sanctuary, rolling meadows, wooded hillsides, and an amazing variety of vegetation. It is a spot undeniably touched by the Divine and was a perfect place to appreciate the current rebirth that was happening all around us.

Marianna and I were strolling leisurely on the boardwalk, chatting and keeping a keen eye on our children, who were riding bikes ahead of us. There were a lot of elderly people enjoying their morning walk, and we were concerned the kids might accidentally bump into one of them. Marianna's youngest child, Melissa, was in a stroller and my younger daughter, Allison, who was only three, was walking along with my sister and me.

The air was crisp and intoxicating, filled with the pungent fragrance of sea salt and a strong, hearty aroma of the hot coffee we were sipping. We chatted about our lives, upcoming plans and things we had recently done. Every now and then we just enjoyed the silence of that sacred space, interrupted only by the rhythmic pounding of the waves on the shore or the joyful squeal of a jubilant child, so happy to run free after a long cold winter. The beach was mostly empty, as it was a little too soon for sunbathing. However, the rocky shoreline was dotted with a few solitary fishermen casting their lines, as the waves churned around their high rubber boots that allowed them to wade a few feet out into the surf.

I'm not sure how many minutes had passed since we started our walk when I suddenly realized that Allison was not next to me. I looked behind us; she wasn't there! I looked toward the water as waves of terror crashed mercilessly over me. I envisioned her being swept away into a dark watery tomb. My heart began pounding so hard it had a loud audible sound that echoed throughout my entire body.

"Oh my God, Allison, she's gone. I can't see her anywhere," I shrieked. "I can't see her anywhere. Marianna, please watch Jake and Bri. I'm going to head back toward the parking lot."

"Go, go, go," she shouted, noticeably sharing my panic and fear.

I turned and sprinted as fast as I could, constantly scanning my periphery, hoping and praying I would see my beautiful blond-haired, blue-eyed baby girl. Backtracking, the boardwalk was a long straightaway until you made a slight left turn that led to a tunnel housing the restrooms and concession. Beyond that was the parking lot.

"Dear God, please, please keep my baby safe. Protect her from harm and please let me find her," I pleaded. Adrenalin and absolute horror were the only fuel that enabled my trembling legs to move my body forward.

I made the turn toward the tunnel and parking lot. Thoughts of abduction and being brutally hit by a car shot like gunfire into my anguished mind.

"Allison," I suddenly screamed as I saw her on the left side of the boardwalk. She was happily playing and climbing on a railing, seemingly unaffected by having been separated from me—very strange since she was extremely attached to me all the time. Standing next to her was an elderly man with a short, silver beard. He was wearing white cotton pants, a blue button-down shirt, a white sport jacket, and a white fedora. He was not interacting with her at all. He just seemed to be watching over her, protecting her and keeping her safe.

"I was just waiting for you to come back," he crooned softly as if he had been somehow certain I would return.

His voice was calm and soothing. His eyes were aqua-colored blue, clear, and transparent like a beautiful mountain stream. In only the small second that I saw him, his eyes seemed to silently and mysteriously hint of a gentle inner peace, revealing the open doorway to his kind and loving soul.

I turned and scooped up my little girl into my arms, holding her as tightly as I could. Tears of relief and gratitude washed over me, cleansing away the previous moments of foreboding. No more than ten seconds had passed. I turned to offer my sincere and heartfelt thanks to that wonderful man for having protected my precious child. He was gone! He had simply vanished! I looked all around, certain I would spot him since I doubted any other man would be dressed as he was. He was nowhere. He hadn't gone to the parking lot because I had been facing in that direction. We walked back to the main boardwalk and scanned from east to west and down the beach—nothing. Suddenly, in a moment that is now frozen in time for me, I completely understood. I reached down and picked Allison up again and held her, this time more gently and much more relaxed.

"Honey, that man was an angel," I whispered softly into her tiny ear. "When I couldn't find you I prayed for God to protect you and keep you safe. He answered my prayer and sent one of his heavenly angels to watch over you. We received a very special gift today and an incredible miracle." I don't think she really understood any of what I was saying, but she could feel my joy and see me smile. She smiled too. I lifted my head and looked toward the clear blue sky and beyond, into heaven's celestial realm.

"Thank you, dear sweet angel. I will, forever, be grateful and I will never forget you. The memory of you will stay with me for the rest of my life and perhaps someday we will meet again."

> "ANGELS ARE EVERYWHERE READY
> AND WAITING TO COME TO OUR AID
> OR TO GUIDE US ON OUR PATH.
> ALL THAT IS NECESSARY TO RECEIVE
> THEIR ASSISTANCE IS A SIMPLE
> PRAYER. ANGELS COME IN
> MANY FORMS. THEY MAY EVEN
> WEAR WHITE FEDORAS!"

# Morning Fairies

"*B*ri," I whispered as my little girl lay peacefully in bed, still enveloped in the mysterious world of dreams and mystical adventures. "It's an amazing morning. I made some hot cocoa for you. Wait till you see them! They're brighter and more beautiful than ever."

Brianne opened her eyes slowly, stretched her arms over her head, yawned, silently grabbed her blanket, and followed me. She was always so tranquil in the mornings—a lot like me—my other two children—well, not so much. Jake and Allison were definitely not morning people so we just let them sleep while Bri and I shared our magical mother-daughter time together.

I had already put the coffee and hot chocolate out on the patio table, along with a nice warm blanket for me. I pulled open the sliding glass doors and we stepped out into the chilly late spring air. I sat down in the chair that faced east. Brianne climbed up on my lap and we wrapped the blankets tightly around us. She fit perfectly in the little nook inside my arms, as her seven-year-old body was just the right size for cuddling.

The patio wasn't much to look at—just an old slab of weathered cement covered with unruly grass and weeds that relentlessly continued breaking through the many cracks and crevices. In the center was a big, old, red brick fireplace that I'm sure, was once upon a time, functional. But now it was also a place where wandering seeds from neighboring trees, floated aimlessly on the wind, eventually finding their way to that perfect stationary flower pot.

"Good morning grandfather and grandmother trees," I playfully sang as I did most every morning.

Beyond the patio, in the farthest corners stood two large trees. They were different but I couldn't really tell you what kind they were. The one on the left had a bigger trunk, was taller, its leaves were broader, its branches bushier, and it just had a grandfatherly feel about it. We built a massive tree house in his arms that he steadfastly held with pride. The tree on the right was smaller, with a narrow trunk and leaves shaped like teardrops. It had a much more feminine energy so of course she had to be the grandmother. There they stood, greeting us each morning and watching over us all through our days. They provided a natural playground for the children and a wonderful cool, shady spot for me to read, write, or meditate during all of those sultry summer afternoons.

"Look, Mom, there they are."

"They sure are. Wow, they're pretty frisky this morning. Looks like they are celebrating something awfully special or maybe they're just happy to see us."

I held Brianne closer and we looked up at the glowing yellow fireball that was ascending higher and higher into the early morning sky. As we watched with awe and wonder, tiny sparks of colored lights flew out and away from somewhere deep within the core of that flaming celestial body. These colorful sparks looked alive as they streaked rapidly across the heavens. For us, they were alive. We followed them with our eyes until they faded away, only to be followed by another, and another, and another.

"I love the 'morning fairies,'" Bri exclaimed excitedly. "They make me feel happy."

"Me too, honey, and you know what?" She turned her head around and looked up into my eyes.

"God, she is so beautiful!" I thought, and for just a moment I found myself lost in, and swept away by, the unconditional love radiating from her open and loving heart.

"I don't want you ever to forget these incredible mornings that we shared together. When you grow up into the beautiful young woman I know you will be, and when you begin to grow old and a time comes when you may not be able to see me anymore, always remember the 'morning fairies.' Whenever you are enjoying a gorgeous sunrise just like this one and the morning fairies appear, I will be there with you, holding you in my arms, loving you with my heart and assuring you that I will always be with you."

I remembered thinking, at the time, "that was a lot for a little seven-year-old child to take in," but Brianne knew me. She always patiently allowed the poet and philosopher in me to express things she usually didn't understand, and she really didn't have any desire to do so at the time. She was also used to my desire, in special moments like these, to stop time and make a memory that would never fade with the passing years. I hoped, that day, that she would remember our special mornings and never forget how much I love her, even when the day came that I could no longer tell her.

One day years later, when she was in middle school, I found an English paper she had written about the morning fairies. It was an assignment about "her favorite childhood memory." I read the story slowly, cherishing every word and visualizing every detail as she recalled it and described it beautifully. As I finished reading the last words, time once again stood still, and I made another cherished memory for *me* that I placed gently into every corner of my overflowing heart. I brought the paper up and held it to my breast, as tears slipped silently from beneath my closed eyes and I whispered to myself, "I love you too, Bri."

"TIME PASSES QUICKLY
AND OUR CHILDREN GROW UP
IN THE BLINK OF AN EYE.
STAYING IN THE MOMENT,
CREATING SPECIAL MEMORIES
AND PLANTING THEM
IN THE FERTILE SOIL
OF OUR LOVING HEARTS
WILL ALLOW LOVE
TO LIVE FOREVER."

# *Better Days*

*J*anuary 1, 1995—Happy New Year! There was very little to be happy about that day. I had worked the night before at a local restaurant and rang in the start of the New Year serving a large gathering of very festive and slightly tipsy patrons. As I watched all of the kisses and warm embraces filter through the room, I couldn't help but contemplate the sadness of my life and the grief from my slowly dying dreams.

The reality of the end of my marriage had finally rooted itself, and the never-ending drama was beginning to engulf and devour every moment of my life, and my children's lives. I wondered if Jake felt the same way. The kids were nine, eight, and five at the time, and were caught up in the middle of a very messy custody battle that would drag on for another year and a half.

It was 6:00 p.m. I was tired. I was always tired, it seemed. The tension in the house was thick and felt as if it had the consistency of dark, gooey molasses. Trying to move through it took tremendous effort, and trying to escape from it, was impossible. I decided to order pizza for dinner so I wouldn't have to cook. I was trying, all the time, to hide my fear, sadness, and pain from my children, which drained even more of my energy. Yet I had to. It was my job to protect them and make sure they had some happy memories. I hoped that some day they might have at least one or two that would make them smile, not cringe with regret or weep with remorse.

We were all gathered in the kitchen. As I was cutting the pizza, I was suddenly aware that Jake was no longer in the kitchen with us. I couldn't see him or hear him. I turned and headed into the living room. He was there rifling through my pocketbook. I wasn't sure why. I thought perhaps, he was trying to find documents or something that he could use as evidence in the custody case. I don't remember if he found anything that he thought he could use, but I felt upset and very much violated by his actions.

My heart started to pound like a giant sledge hammer in my chest. My body began to tremble and I was overwhelmed by an erupting volcano of hot molten fear. Was my fear rational? I didn't know. However, I was beginning to realize that once engaged in the court system, nothing much makes sense.

"I can't take any more of this," I thought hopelessly. "I'm tired, worn out and so sad."

My internal dialogue continued, "You can't be tired. You can't give up. You have to stay on your toes all the time. The battle lines are drawn. That's how this crazy game of fighting for custody goes. You need to stay alert. The worst thing you can do is to fall apart, lose control, breakdown."

"But I don't want to fight. I hate to fight,"

"If you don't fight you will lose."

I walked quickly over to Jake. I tried to grab my pocketbook from him. I told him to give it to me or I'd call the police. He lifted his head slowly. He glared up at me. His eyes seemed to turn a dark, icy black. I pulled back and raced for the phone. He was beginning to frighten me. He grabbed the phone from me just as the 911 operator answered. I don't remember exactly what he said to them but when Jake hung up the phone, I knew the police were on their way.

I felt so alone and afraid. The police came and listened to Jake's allegations about me. I tried to stay calm as I told them what happened. My body's version of the "perfect storm" was raging inside of me, but I captained my vessel like a cool-headed commander, never showing the blinding, turbulent terror that was consuming me.

The police listened and when we were both finished they told us that it was not a good idea for us to be in the same house that night. They suggested I take the kids and stay elsewhere.

That was it … the last straw. I decided that I had to get out. I wasn't sure anymore what Jake might do. I had to escape the craziness or we'd all be damaged beyond repair. The next day I returned home after he left for work and spent hours on the phone trying to locate a women's shelter. It seemed like my only option at the time. I found one called "Better Days." I gathered together some clothes and my kids, and we left.

We arrived at the shelter in the late afternoon. After the initial processing, we settled into a small bedroom with bunkbeds. I remember looking around and wondering, "How did I get here in my life?" I took a deep breath and it occurred to me that it didn't matter. What mattered was that we finally had some peace.

Not for long! Somehow, some way, he knew immediately where we were. Later the following day, I was informed by the staff at "Better Days" that I had been ordered to appear in court at 9:00 a.m. the next morning or I'd be arrested. They told me that he had gone before the judge with serious accusations about something he said I did the night police were called to the house. I've chosen to omit the details because again, my purpose for writing this book is not to hurt anyone. It is about my choices and what I learned from them. I want my story to be blameless, and most of all, positive and hopefully inspiring.

"My God, what lengths will he go to?" I wondered. "How could anyone possibly believe that I could do this? If they knew me at all, they would know I would never, ever be capable of such a thing. But they don't know me. What if they really do believe him? What if they take away my children?" I wailed in my tortured mind. Fear began engulfing me like an enormous, deadly tsunami promising to cause unavoidable destruction.

I was taken to court by officials of the shelter the following morning. When I arrived, Jake was there. I looked at him sadly and wondered what had happened to us. How had we come to this terrible place?

"I can't hear this case right now," the judge explained. "I have a child abuse case on the docket which takes precedence. I will try to hear your case at 2:00 p.m. In the meantime, based on the evidence before me, I am awarding full, temporary custody to Mr. Mainer. Mrs. Mainer, you are to go back to the shelter and get your three children and deliver them to your husband by 12:00 noon. Should you refuse to do so; a warrant will be issued for your arrest." The gavel went down and the judge left the courtroom as I silently screamed, "You can't. It's all a big lie. I didn't do anything. How can you take my babies?" I stood there frozen in time, completely shocked, devastated, demoralized, defeated, and so, so alone. My tears felt like hot sticky blood dripping from a mortal, open wound. My life force was draining from my body. I couldn't survive this. But I had to survive. I had to for my kids."

I did return the children to my husband, just as the judge ordered. Jake seemed to be reveling in victory and completely unmoved by my obvious emotional pain and anguish.

We went back to court at 2:00 p.m. The judge did hear the case and in the end, he found that I was not guilty of the accusations. However, he also ordered that neither of us could remove the children from the marital home.

I had to go back home and live in the same house with Jake. How could we possibly live together after all of this? I felt exhausted and numb and at the same time I was reeling in a pain that coursed through the deepest most intimate parts of my body and tore massive, gaping holes in the grid-work of my soul's light.

"Had God abandoned me? No, He didn't. Surely He was the reason it didn't end up worse. It wasn't over. Did I have anything left in me to fight with? I had to. I just needed to rest and try to process what happened, why it happened, how I handled it or didn't handle it, and what I learned. I would find a way to survive this terrible time. I would find the strength. I would fight but I would fight in my own way with weapons made of truth, light, and faith. I would release fear and replace it with affirmations shouting of, and calling for, the divine design for my life—for all of our lives. I would choose peace even though the world I was living in felt like a war; God, help me."

We left the courthouse and as we did my husband stopped and turned toward me, acting as if we had just been to a great sporting event and very matter-of-factly said, "So, how about we go get the kids and we'll all go out for a nice dinner."

"Surely he's kidding. He's not kidding." I raised my head and looked deeply into his eyes hoping to see even a glimpse of regret or remorse. I didn't see it, only a look of triumph. I suppose he accomplished what he had set out to do. I was back in the house. Maybe Jake was just as sad as I was about what had become of our life and our marriage, but he couldn't or wouldn't show it. I slowly lowered my head shaking it from side to side. I turned and headed toward my car. The sadness and sorrow was like heavy, metal armor weighing me down and making each step a struggle. I was acutely aware that there was much more to come, so I had better thicken my skin, dig in my heels, and get ready for what I was sure would be, the biggest, ugliest fight of my life.

"EVEN WITH PEACE AS MY
MANTRA AND ULTIMATE GOAL
IN MY LIFE, I HAVE LEARNED
THAT, AT TIMES, I MUST RISE UP
AND BRING FORTH THE WARRIOR
WOMAN INSIDE OF ME. YET, WHEN
I AM CALLED TO DO SO, I CHOOSE
ONLY WEAPONS, OF TRUTH, LIGHT,
AND AN UNWAVERING FAITH AND
BELIEF THAT THERE IS A GREATER
PERFECTION AT WORK THAT I
CANNOT ALWAYS SEE."

As the divorce and custody battled dragged on and on, many times I would escape alone to the beauty and tranquility of the ocean's shore. Somehow, it calmed me and I could find a moment of peace there. One day, however, I was feeling completely overwhelmed and engulfed by the pain and tragedy of my situation. I sat, grief-stricken, with my journal and pen in hand hoping to find some answers. What came forth, however, were not answers; at least it didn't seem so at the time. What tumbled forth was a manifestation of the helplessness that was consuming me, as well as feelings of being swallowed up and destroyed by the endless attacks on my soul—my spirit.

Here is what I wrote on that dark and very sad day.

# The Unsuspecting Lover

I sense that deep within these tranquil waters
That beckon so alluringly,
Lies a strange mystery, an untamed power
And a frightening evil.

The words I write flow freely from another source:
The troubled souls of many an unsuspecting lover.
They once felt as I do now, as I sit and watch
The rolling curls
And listen peacefully to the muffled roar
*(a thousand voices in disguise)*
That this is life's tranquilizer.

Here I can escape with a sense of endlessness
And feel a strange power of incredible magnitude.
I find myself here at the end of the earth
Running blindly from all that is too frightening
Or overwhelming to bear,
And it is here that he coos and beckons
With all of his wondrous beauty.

He calms and soothes and utilizes his love potions
That he offers in the shapes of graceful birds,
Endless stretches of pure white sand,
The warming rays of the sun,
And his cooling waters with massive arms
That refresh and caress my body, sometimes rendering me helpless.

Yet, with a sense of peace and tranquility
I know that at any moment all of his beauty
Can transform into a chilling dark abyss.
The light and the warmth of the sun disappear.
His once tender touch then hurls me wildly in all directions
As I fight madly to free myself from his clutches.
Yet, as my strength weakens and my will to live quickly fades,
His strength seems to intensify
His power reaches maddening heights …

His waters then calm themselves and it is clear
That his potions have succeeded once again,
And his strength has been renewed by still one more ...
*Unsuspecting lover!*

"MY PEN AND MY LOVE OF
WRITING, MANY TIMES, FIND A WAY
TO RELEASE FROM INSIDE OF ME
WHAT I OTHERWISE COULD NOT."

"IN A ROMANTIC RELATIONSHIP,
I WILL ALWAYS MAKE SURE THAT
BENEATH THE SEDUCTION OF
PASSION AND DESIRE LIES THE
ENDURING COMMITMENT OF
FRIENDSHIP AND RESPECT!"

# *Angel in a Blue Corvette*

*O*ur unbelievable three-and-a-half year divorce, custody battle, and pursuant three-month trial was indeed, a nightmare, and much of what happened to me seemed unjust and unfair. Yet, many times the court system is anything but fair. As I stated earlier, I will not go into tremendous detail about the specific circumstances. It is very important to me that everyone understands my intention for writing this book is to heal and help, not to hurt or wound anyone. Again, this book is about my choices, my response to the life I created, both the good and the difficult, and how I learned from it. I also want to protect my children from any possible adverse affects from this book project as well. They have already lived through the intricate details of the ordeal once, and I don't want them to have to relive them again.

As I have said, I thought the decision to leave my marriage would have been the hardest thing I would ever do in my life; I was wrong! I never imagined the craziness and turmoil that would ensue. I never thought I would be fighting such an awful battle for custody of my children.

During the three-month custody trial, my personal journals and spiritual life were paraded through the halls of the courthouse as if they were evidence of evil and insanity. Jake's attorney read them daily until, thankfully, the judge demanded that he stop. Day in and day out I struggled to stay positive and have faith that in the end everything would be OK, and I would have my children with me. I felt as if I was being pushed over the edge emotionally at every moment, and I teetered on that precarious edge for three long months.

Much to my disbelief at the beginning of the trial, none of the people in place, who were to decide custody, believed me when I tried to tell them who I really was. I was so infuriated about how Jake's attorney was trying to make me look like someone I was not, just to win the case. Yet, I couldn't seem to muster up the appropriate anger or outrage at Jake—only forgiveness. That didn't make sense to anyone, even me. One explanation is that it was just my nature—the person I was and continue to be. Another was that maybe it was simply part of my Christian upbringing, to love and forgive as Jesus did, no matter what. I still have no real answers for this; but love always feels better than hate to me.

The whole custody ordeal was surreal. I had always hated confrontation and completely avoided it. I didn't know how to fight. I believed that truth and my faith were all I needed to get me through. I was so very wrong. At the beginning of the trial, things did not look good for me. A picture of who I was had been painted, and it did not even resemble the person I really was. So on the first day of trial, there was a forensic psychologist's report recommending that my ex-husband receive custody. The children's lawyer was also leaning in that direction as well. I had been broken, shattered and so filled with sadness and sorrow, that it was crushing me. If it hadn't been for my intense love for my children, I would have given up. For at times, I was certain that I would soon disappear forever into a deep, dark place inside myself just so I could escape the tortuous, unrelenting pain.

A few months before the trial began, my initial attorney petitioned the judge to be released from my case because he had cystic fibrosis. I had no money to hire a new attorney. The judge seemed unmoved by my plight. It was going to trial in a few weeks no matter what, which meant I would have to represent myself. I was terrified. I went to the county's pro bono project (free legal assistance for those with financial need) and the director assured me that she would find someone who would take my case. I went to several attorneys and they declined. I suppose it looked too hopeless and impossible to win. Then, a man named Wesley Grogan III agreed to see me. I sat in his office as he quietly read over and pondered the mounds of papers, including the damaging forensic report. I sat there silently, yet wanting to scream and cry, tell him how unjust all of this was, and beg him to please, please, please help me. I didn't. I simply prayed. He placed the papers on his desk, took off his glasses, placed them carefully on his desk and looked into my eyes and said, "Something is not right! I'm taking this case." Tears welled in my eyes. I put my hands over my face and I tried with everything I had to hold it together. After a moment, I took a deep breath, I looked up and I asked him only one thing.

"All I want you to do," I implored, "is to bring out the truth. This is not about proving how bad Jake is. It is about revealing who I really am. Even if something is brought up that might hurt my case, I will not lie. I made a promise to myself and to God."

"Done!" he responded.

So began my miracle. Wesley worked tirelessly for no money at all. I called him my angel in a blue corvette—his vehicle of choice. The three months we went to trial was from October to December in 1996, and we won. We won because he did what I had asked. He simply brought out the truth.

It was a horrible painful ordeal. Jake came into the courthouse daily with huge boxes piled on top of each other, wheeling it with a luggage carrier. I trembled wondering what in the world could be in there that could prove I was an unfit mother. I think he was just trying to intimidate and unravel me. If he was, he came close. Maybe Jake hadn't intended for things to get so out of control. I've learned that once lawyers are involved, it almost always gets nasty in divorce and custody cases. As the days wore on and many of the people who supported me testified, it became more and more clear that things were turning around, and I was going to win custody of my children.

After the trial ended, I wrote a letter to the pro bono project telling them how wonderful Mr. Grogan had been and to thank them for all of their help. Shortly after that, Mary Pirini, the director of the project, called me.

"Drusilla, this is Mary Pirini. I'm calling to tell you that Mr. Grogan has won an award. He is being honored as attorney of the month for the work he did on your case a few months ago. There will be a dinner at a local hotel and I would like to know if you would do a speech for him and tell your story."

"Although I would love to, Mary," I responded. "I have never given a public speech and just the thought of it scares me to death."

"Your letter was so eloquent, beautiful and heartfelt," she replied. "I am sure you will do a great job."

"Just because I can write, doesn't mean I can give a good speech," I countered. "However, I will do it for Mr. Grogan. I owe him at least that much. I will do my best."

The night of the dinner came. I arrived all alone, and as I walked toward the conference room I heard various people whispering "She's here, she's here."

"Uh oh," I thought, "Something is definitely up."

"Mary, who else is giving speeches tonight besides me," I inquired, thinking that there were many other attorneys being honored that night besides Wesley, so surely there would be others speaking.

"Daniel Vassel, a local state politician," she informed me.

"And me?" I gasped, frozen in fear.

"You'll be fine," she calmly assured me.

"Fine?" I questioned silently, in complete shock. "There are two hundred judges and lawyers here and ME. She's got to be kidding! How am I going to get through this? Maybe I should just sneak out."

I didn't, of course. I had nothing written down, no notes at all. I intended to speak from my heart. So I sat down, calmed myself and decided that was what I would do. That's all I had. I needed to tell my story and I wanted to honor Wes. When Daniel Vassel finished his polished, perfect speech, I was introduced. As I walked to the podium everyone in the room was chatting amongst themselves paying little or no attention to me. After all, I was a nonentity in the legal community. I adjusted the microphone and began. My voice was calm, steady, passionate, and strong. I didn't cry. I delivered my words with clarity and authenticity. I truthfully told my story. About one and a half minutes into the speech, the energy in the room was transformed. You could have heard a pin drop. I could actually feel a stream of energy directed towards me as everyone was riveted on the edge of their seats by my tale of injustice and then ultimate triumph.

I concluded the speech by saying the following: "I'd like to end by saying something that Oprah Winfrey said at the end of her *beef trial.*" She said, "You spend your whole life trying to define who you are and then you go into a court of law and there is someone there trying to take that apart piece by piece."

"I felt like that happened to me, but Wesley Grogan not only gave me custody of my children but he put all those pieces back together again, and he gave me back myself."

With that, the room exploded with an uproarious, thunderous standing ovation. Mr. Grogan came running onto the stage and screamed "Who are you anyway?" I wasn't sure. It almost felt as if divine energy descended on me and guided me as I spoke.

What a moment! We were the stars of the night. Judge Connolly, prominent in the county, came up to me afterward and said, "I spend every day in my courtroom listening to speeches by attorneys and I have never heard such an incredible speech. You're in the wrong line of work."

Daniel Vassel asked to have a picture taken with me and Wes. Wes was so proud and so grateful. I was grateful as well for everything: for Wes coming into my life, for that amazing night, and for all I had gained through my struggle over the last several years. I survived! I fought for my children! I fought for me. I fought for truth and justice, and I won. Within myself I found a strong, peaceful, warrior woman who would never again give away her power to anyone. Today, fifteen years later, I am grateful to the man, my ex-husband, who showed me how strong I really am. I have learned over and over that our greatest adversaries are, indeed, our greatest teachers. He taught me well. The trials and the tribulation during that difficult time are part of the fiber of who I have become and a reminder of the beautiful soul I have always been. Those intricate, painful threads will forever remain woven into the beautiful tapestry of my incredible life.

"FEAR IS THE ENEMY OF FAITH.
ONCE FAITH BECOMES
STRONGER THAN ANY FEARS
AND YOU BEGIN
TO VISUALIZE AND BELIEVE
IN YOUR DESIRED OUTCOME,
YOU WILL MANIFEST
WHAT YOU WISHED FOR."

"ANGELS CONTINUE TO COME
IN MANY FORMS FOR ME,
THEY EVEN DRIVE
BLUE CORVETTES."

# Vehicle for Healing and Light

## Introduction to Vehicle for Healing and Light

*W*hen I was in the darkest part of the divorce and custody nightmare, feeling completely overwhelmed, hopeless, and fully absorbed in my own drama, someone very close to me at the time gave some very good advice. He told me the quickest, surest way to heal myself would be to reach out and heal others. I wondered how in the world I could heal anyone when I felt so wounded and so incredibly broken. However, I took this person's advice. Remembering the prayer of the small child, little Dru, who only wanted to serve God, I tried to find a way to do just that, hoping somewhere through my desire to heal others, the healing I so desperately needed for myself would emerge.

In 1995, the beginning of the end of my marriage and in the midst of the horror, I decided to go to school for massage therapy. Through a series of synchronicities and with a renewed sense of purpose, I made up my mind that I would find a way to be of service for God. I reaffirmed the prayer from my childhood: "God, how may I serve? Help me to find a way." I pushed aside those doubts that said you are too fragile and damaged to help anyone and believed that God indeed says, "Come to me now with all of your pain and dysfunction because you are perfect for what I need you to do."

That time in massage school, although it was extremely difficult to balance everything I was going through in my personal life, my children, my custody fight, and my class schedule, it turned out to be a godsend. The school was my sanctuary away from the chaos of my home life. The people I met there cared about me and held me up when I was about to crash violently to the ground allowing my life force to bleed profusely from the open gaping wounds caused by unending despair, helplessness, and pain. They listened with compassion as I cried bitter tears, over what seemed to me, like a terrible injustice in the court system. They helped me believe in myself again and to see and remember the beautiful light *I am* in the many difficult moments when it was hard to remember.

Being in school again, taking on a tough curriculum packed full of western and eastern sciences, and acing just about every class did wonders for my self-esteem. All of the harsh accusations from my husband about how inadequate and "less than" I was, began to fade away. I started to remember my self-worth and my confidence rose. It was then I vowed to take back my power and strength that I had unknowingly given away. I can't deny that every single day was a struggle; it was, but I could finally see a light at the end of a dark and frightening void that had trapped me for far too long.

The custody trial ended in December, 1996 and I graduated from massage school in May, 1997. Though my children and I were traumatized, wounded and facing an uncertain future, we had each other, and we were determined to make it on our own and build a life together. The words from that wise man, who advised me to be of service in order to heal myself, played over and over in my mind. I began each day with those five simple words; "God how may I serve?" He showed me each and every day how, and I followed the guidance of God, my spirit guides, and the angels, as well as my own intuitive voice. We all began to heal; me, my children and so many people who crossed my path, winding up in my treatment room, and allowing me to share my love, wisdom, and "gifts of spirit" with them.

This section, *Vehicle of Healing and Light,* is filled with stories of all of those people and of the miracles that occurred as I offered my life, my work, and my soul to God. Most occurred in my massage treatment room. However, a few of them are about people in my life who have gone through difficult times and made choices that led to amazing miracles, beautiful insights, awe-inspiring wisdom, and amazing enlightenment. I hope you enjoy them. As you read these stories, think about the times when you reached out to a fellow human being in a spirit of help and healing. How did it feel? Are you in a field where you are able to openly and directly help others in their lives? Think about the times you may have had a dramatic affect on someone's life or even when someone has affected yours. Write about it and what you learned from the experience. If you feel your line of work does not offer you the opportunity to be a healing light for others, perhaps you should rethink that. Everyone who crosses your path provides an opportunity for you to reveal to them your beautiful, loving, forgiving, and kind soul. Even the ones who are difficult, annoying or hostile can be touched and transformed by your meeting that negativity with a positive smile, understanding, forgiveness, and compassion. Think perhaps, about how you might change your attitude about the work you do and how you could use the light of your soul to make a difference in the lives of others. Then try it. You will be amazed at how good it feels and how healing it is for you. You might also consider that you may need to make a career change in order for you to follow your life's purpose and feel your bliss. Take some time to meditate and pray about this before making a decision.

Write about miracles that happened in the past when you acted upon the call to serve, or were served by others; or write about those happening in the present with your new awareness. Hopefully, you will share them with me and together we can dissolve much of the anger, fear and intolerance, and replace it with forgiveness, love, and service.

# Called to Serve

*B*usiness was slow that night. The whole staff was waiting around dressed in neatly pressed tuxedos and crisp white shirts hoping that at least a few customers would venture out for dinner. There were only two females in a wait staff, which primarily consisted of Italian men— appropriate, since the restaurant where I worked was a five-star Italian restaurant. So Charlene, the only other female, and I, spent a lot of time talking about what was going on in our lives. That night the subject of my spiritual life came up and she asked me a lot of questions about energy healing, psychic healing, auras, etc.

"You should become a massage therapist," she exclaimed out of nowhere.

"Why would you say that?" I asked.

"Every massage therapist I've ever met is just like you," she replied. "You know, talking about all that metaphysical stuff. You'd fit right in."

"Hmmm, that's a thought," I responded. "I've never even had a massage, though. I don't know if I would like it, or even be good at it. I am looking for another profession, though—one that could give me more satisfaction and a truer sense of purpose. I also need to have a job that would allow me to be home with my kids at night and on weekends. Besides, now that Jake and I are divorcing and he's fighting me for custody, I think he might use my being in the restaurant business as one way to prove that he should have primary custody. Maybe massage therapy *is* the answer to a lot of questions."

Those words that Charlene uttered that night became a tiny seed that began to germinate in the shadowed corners of my mind. The tiny seed grew and developed until it was almost all I thought about; that is when I wasn't caring for the children or going to court proceedings. Maybe massage therapy would help me have a joyful ending for my life story, which at present, was filled with more fear than joy and abundance. I researched local schools, and I found one not too far from where we lived.

One morning I called the school and made an appointment for a tour of the facility to consider applying for acceptance if I liked what I saw. I got in my car and began the forty-five minute drive to the campus. During the entire trip a conflict was going on inside of me between my logical, rational mind, and my idealistic and passionate heart.

"Why are you bothering with this whole thing? You know there is no money left in the bank account. Your credit is really awful now that the house is in foreclosure. You'll never be able to get any financial aid, so how in the world do you think you will pay for this?"

"Don't worry about the details. It will be OK," encouraged my more childlike, trusting side. "Trust the intuitive feeling you have that says you should pursue this and that everything will work out perfectly. You have to believe in yourself and have confidence that your soul and your heart will lead you on the correct path—the path that God wants for you."

"Whatever you say, but I think you're nuts. It will never happen," retorted my more cynical persona.

"Fine, I hear you but just keep your negative thoughts to yourself. I'm going to do this with or without your support or approval."

"OK but when you get your hopes up and everything doesn't work out just remember …"

"I know, I know you told me so," I responded.

After a tour of the school and a discussion with an admissions advisor, I was impressed and excited. Just being there filled me with anticipation and a determination to find a way to realize the goal of going to school for massage therapy. I also felt a sense of familiarity as I walked through the halls and viewed the classrooms, the clinics, and herbal laboratory; almost as if I had done this work before. I felt a connection to people I had never met, at least not so far in this lifetime. I knew, absolutely, that this was where I needed and wanted to be. I believed there was a divine energy guiding me and that all that had happened so far was not a coincidence but a remarkable display of synchronicity and perfection. Even my argumentative mind seemed to sense that massage school would be the vehicle that would help me to be of service to others, and to God. If this was indeed God's Will, He would find a way to make it happen. The pessimistic part of me, only trying to protect me, was silent as my excitement grew and my energy expanded beyond the walls of the building out into every part of the universe. It was awesome.

I left that day sure that I would somehow find a way to pay for it. However, my enthusiasm and confidence began to wane as I tried to figure out how God could make this work out. Money was money and all the desire in the world wouldn't matter if I couldn't find a way to finance it. I decided that I just needed to have faith. As I meditated one day I remembered something that a woman in the financial aid office at the school told me. She told me that there is a state program that provides vocational and educational services for individuals with disabilities. I have a pretty severe hearing disability so I thought just maybe that would be the answer.

As I researched the program I found that they did not necessarily provide funding for school. It was entirely up to your counselor. Sometimes they just found you another position that was more adaptable to your particular disability. Yet, it seemed like it was my only hope. I had to believe that I had been directed this far for a reason so I had to follow through. I was told that the process of working through the program would take months from start to finish.

I arrived at the office in October, 1995. There were several other people there with me also applying for assistance. First we had a group meeting. The representative explained what we could expect from the process. He told us that it is a program funded by The State Education Department. The next step after this meeting, he informed us, was that we were to meet with a counselor individually to discuss our personal goals and objectives.

Mr. John Canary, my counselor, was an elderly gentleman who was kind and soft spoken. His office was simple but not very organized. He sat at a large oak desk, the surface of which was barely visible from all of papers scattered all over it. I sat in a chair beside him. He began by telling me he was about to retire and that I would be one of his last cases. He asked me who Drusilla was and what she wanted her life to be—what she wanted her legacy to be. I thought for a moment or two when suddenly a strange, warm sensation came over me. I felt an itchy, tingling feeling on the top of my head and words began to flow from my lips. I don't remember even thinking about what I was saying. The words just came, as if from another place. I felt inspired. I expressed my complete truth, my dreams and aspirations, and I did so with passion and enthusiasm. As I was speaking, I was also listening to how eloquently and clearly I spoke.

"Was this really only me speaking," I wondered, "or was I being given help and inspiration from a Divine source."

I told him how I have always wanted to be a vehicle for healing and light. I shared with him that it is extremely important to me to be of service to my fellow human beings, and to God. I assured him that my intentions were honorable and principled. I wanted to become a licensed massage therapist. Doing so would enable me to touch people's lives in a meaningful way, and I wanted to make a positive difference in the world. I reassured him that if he helped me he would not be disappointed, and he would never regret the time and resources the program invested in me.

When I finished, my face was bright red and flushed. Every cell in my body felt like dancing flames of an eternal, internal fire that would never die out. *I* was that fire and I knew it was ignited by a memory of a predetermined path I had chosen long ago. Mr. Canary listened quietly and carefully to every word I spoke.

Softly he questioned, "When does the next class begin?" "Well, tomorrow," I replied. "However, the class after that begins in January."

He looked deeply and seriously into my eyes. Very slowly the corners of his mouth turned upward as he smiled and nodded his head a few times. He picked up the phone and placed the receiver to his ear.

"I'm calling the school and giving them a verbal approval over the phone. You start classes tomorrow. I believe in you. I believe you *will* make a difference. We will pay for all your expenses: tuition, books, massage table, and supplies. Whatever you need, just have the school charge it to us. This is a full grant not a loan."

There were no words that came then. None seemed adequate. My gratitude was overwhelming. I sat stunned trying to process what he had said. Tears of hope and renewal fell like morning dew dripping from a glorious spring flower, opening to the birth of a new day. I was about to embark on a magnificent, mystical journey.

"I MUST ALWAYS TRUST
IN THE DIVINE DESIGN FOR MY LIFE.
FOR IF MY DREAMS AND VISIONS
ARE PART OF
MY PRE-BIRTH PLANNING
AND THEREFORE MY LIFE PURPOSE,
GOD WILL FIND A WAY
EVEN WHEN THERE SEEMS TO BE
NO WAY TO MAKE IT HAPPEN."

# *Gifts of Spirit*

*F*or any of us who have chosen to work in any healing capacity with the sincere intention of cooperating with Divine energy, we know that "Gifts of Spirit" grow quickly. This amazing work provides me with some of the most rewarding and fulfilling moments of my life. I have come to understand something very essential, however. In order to continue receiving these gifts and performing this extraordinary work, I must always be sure to remove my very proud, and at times, needy ego from the equation. My guides are very clear about the fact that I am a vehicle for healing and not the healer. Divine energy moves through me and washes over me like waves of golden sunshine on a warm summer day.

Today I am comfortable and at ease with the sometimes abrupt messages or visions that appear and fade as I work. It is not unusual for me to put my hands on someone and feel intense emotions such as sadness, sorrow or grief. I often sense childhood issues such as abandonment or abuse. Occasionally, I am aware of a deceased loved one who enters the room and is eager to have me deliver a message. Perhaps the most important lesson I have learned in my practice is discernment. No matter how much I want to ease someone's pain or assist in their healing, it is not always appropriate to do so using the information I receive. I must always put the safety and protection of their soul first. Images and messages that come forth, if given, could sometimes, do more harm than good. At those times I am sad that I cannot do more to ease their hurt. So, I simply offer a fervent prayer that God will touch them and help them to heal.

Traveling back in time to 1997 when I first began practicing as a massage therapist, this was all new to me. I had been seriously journeying and searching on my own spiritual path for years but it had been very solitary. I was just beginning to develop my sensitivity and skills, when into my treatment room walked Jeremy. He was an attractive man in his late forties. He had chestnut brown hair, a well trimmed beard and there was a kind of regalness about him. He was well-dressed, soft spoken, and articulate. I asked him if he had any particular problem.

"My hands hurt all the time," he informed me. "I don't know why. Nothing out of the ordinary has happened. I didn't injure them or anything. It's strange."

"OK," I thought, "this shouldn't be too hard."

As I worked on his forearms and hands I could not see or feel anything obvious. No tightness or spasms in the extensors or flexors and no apparent arthritis in the joints. I did my best. He left the office and returned two weeks later.

"How are your hands, Jeremy?" I inquired.

"They still hurt," he replied with evident frustration in his voice.

"Hmm, OK let's try again," I responded.

Jeremy presented with the same findings and I delivered the same focus and treatment with a slightly more intense pressure. Again, he left and returned two weeks later with the same complaint.

Now, I was the one who was frustrated. As I waited outside the room for him to undress and get onto the table I sought assistance from my spirit guides.

"OK, I need help. What's the problem here? What's up with Jeremy's hands?"

With a bit of shock and surprise I received an immediate response. It felt like a voice inside my head but it was unfamiliar. I knew it was not mine. There was an air of authority in it. Yet, it was kind and gentle.

"There's something in his life that he is holding too tightly. Ask him what it is."

"I don't think so," I respectfully responded in my mind. "He'll think I'm nuts."

Patiently, yet, insistently the words were repeated, "… ask him what it is." OK, I guess I just have to trust what is coming through. Here goes!" I entered the room.

"Jeremy, is there something in your life right now that you may be holding too tightly that you may need to let go of?"

Without hesitation he shot back, "Well my wife, but I'm not letting go of her."

"It may not mean that it is your wife that you need to let go of," I suggested to him gently. "However, there may be something in or surrounding your relationship at this time that you may need to let go of, and trust that the divine design for your life, whatever that is, will unfold."

He then revealed to me that right before he came to see me for the first time, he had found a romantic card tucked away under a jewelry box on his wife's dresser. It was given to her by her boss. Upon confronting her, he learned that she had been having an affair for over six months. They had contemplated divorce but decided to try to work through it. He was so filled with fear on so many levels. He was emotionally holding on to her so tightly that it manifested with pain in his hands.

"Just this awareness, many times, is enough to eliminate the problem and the pain," I assured him. "Just physically open your hands and let it all go. Turn it over and have faith that whatever unfolds will be the divine design."

Jeremy then told me he had very a strong faith in God. At that moment, he revealed that he became acutely aware that fear truly is the enemy of faith. He opened his hands, let go of the fear, and released the pain and uncertainty of the situation to God. He returned two weeks later pain free.

Today, eleven years later, Jeremy still comes to me for massage. He and his wife are still together and happy. He, I'm sure, had no idea that the difficulty in his life would be the very catalyst that would provide me with my first miraculous "Gift of Spirit." It was an amazing and humbling moment for me. Even now, when these wonderful, mystical happenings occur, I am still in awe of the synchronicity. I marvel at the continuous and respective teaching and learning that transpires, between me as a therapist, and my clients, as well as between all human souls every day of our lives. I learn as much as I teach from every person who crosses my path. Each time I receive the honor of being a vehicle for healing and light, I turn my eyes up toward the heavens and silently, in my mind, offer a very simple prayer; "Thank you."

"I KNOW THAT EACH DAY, WITH EACH PERSON I ENCOUNTER, I AM PROVIDED WITH AN OPPORTUNITY TO LEARN SOMETHING OR TO GIVE TO INDIVIDUALS THE WISDOM, TRUTH, AND LOVE THAT RESIDES WITHIN ME. I AM FILLED WITH AWE AND GRATITUDE."

# *Bravo Adam*

*H*is mother brought him to me for a massage when he was only ten years old. I had been treating his mom for quite some time and she had been telling me how concerned she was about her only child, Adam. He just didn't fit in, he had very few friends, and now he was refusing to go to school. His self-esteem was at an all-time low, and psychological counseling wasn't helping.

"Maybe you could teach him some of the spiritual principles that you have taught me," she queried. "Maybe it's his soul that needs tending."

I assured her that I would be glad to help if I could.

I'll never forget the first time he came to me. He walked into my treatment room with his head down, fixated on the floor below. He was short and chubby with bushy, curly blond hair. I asked him some questions and he answered politely, still not lifting his head. It was almost as if he was afraid that if I looked into his eyes they would reveal who he really was or was not, and I wouldn't like what I found. Finally, he did look up. He had the most beautiful eyes but they were filled with sadness. He spoke with such maturity. His vocabulary was so "off-the-charts" that a few times I had to ask him what a word meant. In spite of what appeared to me to be a child with many gifts and talents, his energy revealed a child devoid of any joy or excitement and little or no self-confidence.

I explained to him how to prepare for the treatment. I left and when I came back in I chuckled to myself. He was all over the place. One arm was over his head, and one was hanging off the massage table. One leg was bent and the other was dangling off the table. I straightened him out, fully draped him, and began the treatment. I was doing an Amma Therapy which is an oriental technique that involves the use of acupressure. I pressed on CV 17 which is an acupuncture point on the midline of the body in the center of the chest.

"What's that," he asked abruptly.

"CV 17," I told him.

"No, it's not," he retorted.

"It's not?" I asked.

"No, it's the xyphoid process." he exclaimed.

Sure enough he was absolutely correct. In western anatomy that *is* the location of the xyphoid process, a small cartilaginous extension of the lower part of the sternum.

"What a bright child," I remarked to myself.

I saw and sensed so much potential in him, and at that moment I was committed to helping this young boy to find his joy, learn to love himself, and to remember how magnificent he was and has always been.

Month after month, year after year, Adam would come to see me. At first his mother would bring him. Eventually he got his driver's license, and he came on his own. He came for a massage but what he really came for was to find the answers that would allow him to live a happy and fulfilled life. Adam was the target of a lot of ridicule because of his weight and because he was just plain different from the other kids. He was serious, introspective, intellectual, and oh so negative. The things he said to himself about himself were far worse than any of the things the other kids said about him. We discussed many, many things over the years but there was one main underlying lesson I taught over and over.

"Be careful what you say to yourself in the privacy of your own mind and out loud because those thoughts and words *will* go out into the world and draw into your life people, and experiences to support them.

If you say, *I am fat, I am ugly, I am stupid,* etc.; guess what, Adam, your subconscious mind will go about bringing people into your life who will tell you just that. You are perpetuating your own pain by what you are thinking and saying."

Adam listened. He questioned and doubted me. He debated the spiritual principles we discussed but something kept bringing him back to me. Finally, he started trusting me and what I was trying to teach him more and more. He began testing all the principles, and they began working. His life began to change and for the first time I saw some hope, and he felt hope as well. It was a long hard struggle, however, trying to rewrite his patterns. He always seemed to slip back into the "woe is me" mode. One day, many years ago, I remember getting so frustrated with him. He was spending the whole hour on my massage table having a major pity party.

"Adam, STOP," I commanded sternly. "Here's what I want you to do. I want you to go out and volunteer somewhere. Get out of your own 'stuff' and help others. The best way to heal *you* is to try to heal or help others."

He did! He became an EMT and he is still one today, and at the same time he is studying to be a medic. That decision seemed to change everything for him. His confidence started to grow. His co-workers respected him and truly liked him. The people he was helping showed him gratitude and appreciation, and he found along the way, a sense of humor that was delightful. He finally embraced the fact that he is different and that was a really good thing. He recognized his wonderful qualities of loyalty, honesty, and moral integrity. He started working out, eating healthy foods, and lost a lot of weight. He became far gentler with himself about the things he wanted to change. His self-esteem began to rise.

I remember clearly when he was in his early 20's. He would travel one hour each way from his home to mine every Saturday for a massage but mostly to talk about what was happening in his life and to ponder the spiritual lessons he was learning from his experiences. One Saturday he told me about an EMT call he had received and responded to the previous night, a multiple shooting and fatality. He handled it with strength, courage, and leadership. I was so proud. Before he left my house he walked to the bottom of the stairs, turned, and looked up at me.

"You do know that you changed my life forever don't you," he offered me with sincerity, warmth, and kindness.

Overwhelmed by his remark and feeling so grateful I responded, "No Adam, *you* changed your life forever."

He smiled the most beautiful smile. He turned and left. My eyes filled with tears and I exclaimed out loud, *"BRAVO Adam!"*

"ONE OF THE GREATEST GIFTS
FOR ME IS WHEN I KNOW THAT
I HAVE TOUCHED SOMEONE'S LIFE
IN A POSITIVE WAY.
IF I STAY PRESENT AND
LOOK FOR THESE OPPORTUNITIES,
THEY MIRACULOUSLY APPEAR."

# *Spiritual Partners on a Path*

"**K**ate Cameron," I summoned, holding her client chart in my hand. "That would be me," exploded a bellowing voice from the back of the room. "Be gentle with us; we're both virgins!"

Everyone in the waiting room lifted their heads from the various magazines and books they were reading, astonished to hear such a strange remark. Not much surprised me since I had been practicing massage therapy for a very long time. However, after many years of working with people's energy, I had developed an extra sensory gift that allowed me to see beyond the words and actions of a person to unspoken and sometimes intentionally or unintentionally hidden truth. This was one of those times when that imaginary psychic hat suddenly appeared on my head, and I knew this was going to be "one of those moments!"

Kate was a middle-aged woman about forty-five years old with bleached blond hair. Despite quite a few extra pounds she was sporting, she looked stylish and handsome. She hopped up from her chair, gave a quick kiss on the cheek to the younger woman with whom she had come and then followed me to the treatment room.

"Hi Kate, my name is Drusilla. It's nice to meet you." We proceeded down the hallway as I began gathering information so I could tailor the massage to her particular needs. "I know, from your remark in the waiting room, you have never had a massage before, and I see you checked off neck and shoulder pain on your intake sheet. Is this due to a recent injury or is it something chronic and long term," I questioned in my usual, professional tone.

"You know how it is," she responded delivering a belly laugh that seemed strangely out of place under the circumstances. "I'm getting old. Everything hurts but hey, I don't let it stop me. Life is too much damn fun."

"Good for you! That's a terrific attitude to have," I remarked even though her energy was telling a very different story. I gave her instructions about how to prepare for the massage and then waited outside for her to disrobe and get onto the table.

"So what kind of massage is this?" she inquired as I reentered the room, still in her overly jubilant and boisterous demeanor.

"It is European sometimes called Swedish massage which focuses on circulation and lymph drainage."

"What other kinds of stuff do you do?"

"I practice Amma Therapy which is an oriental technique and focuses on the energy meridians. I also do Reiki, hands on healing. This technique does not offer much tissue manipulation and yet it is a powerful, healing modality. In addition, I read people's energy by focusing on the chakras or the energy system using a pendulum. It is amazing how much information you can receive by doing this particular kind of work; I usually only do readings in conjunction with other treatments."

"Really," she asked, suddenly a bit more serious and very curious. She lifted her head and shoulders from the table, propped her upper body onto her forearms, and stared almost pleadingly into my eyes. "What kind of information are you getting about me?"

I sensed both apprehension and excitement at the same time.

"I assure you, Kate, that I only do this kind of work with the cooperation and consent of the client. I would never invade your personal space or your privacy. If you would like, and with your consent, I will do a reading for you."

"Fire away! I'm ready!"

I centered myself, took several deep, cleansing breaths, said a short prayer asking to be of service, and began.

"There seems to be a discrepancy in the way you present yourself to the world and what is really going on inside of you. Your words and actions portray someone who appears to be happy and joyful, and your sense of humor is infectious and contagious. However, your energy reveals that it is all an illusion, a mask to hide the extraordinarily intense pain buried deep inside of you. When you were twelve or thirteen years old something very traumatic happened to you. You never fully dealt with it and it is deeply affecting your relationships, especially with men. I sense that the trauma had to do with a man."

As I spoke, the previous air of jubilation faded away. Her face transformed horrifically as lines of anguish and heartache gouged deep grooves in her brow, and her expression became twisted and contorted uncovering a woman not at all resembling the one who first stepped into my treatment room.

"I've never told anyone this story before, never! I can't believe I am going to tell you but something is telling me to trust you. When I was thirteen years old I was hanging around with kids much older than me. I thought it was so cool. One day some friends picked me up in a car and said we were going over to this guy Joe's house to hang out. Once we got there, things got out of control. There was a lot of drinking and partying. Towards the end of the night the older kids decided it would be funny to "hook me up" with one of the guys there. They pushed me toward him and he grabbed my arm.

Kate paused a moment, fighting back tears as all of the hideous memories came flooding back.

"They just turned me over to him. I wasn't sure about what was happening but I instinctively knew I didn't want to go with him. He dragged me into a room. I tried to fight him off and get away but I couldn't. Once in the room, he closed the door, locked it and then he brutally raped me. I begged and pleaded with him not to do it but he'd been drinking a lot and didn't listen. I was so scared and so confused. I was just too young to understand but I knew it was … he was … evil and ugly … at least in that moment. I hated him! I hated what he had done to me. Afterward, I think I was in shock. I felt so many awful emotions like horror, fear, and shame, but mostly I felt dirty and really betrayed. I thought they were my friends. How could they have done that to me? I never told anyone about what happened that night. I tried to forget it but it is always just a thought away and I have a lot of trouble trusting anyone, especially men. I am sorry for getting so upset," she apologized. Mournful tears gushed endlessly as the dam that she had constructed with her avoidance and deception gave way to the building pressure. "I don't usually carry on like this."

I gently lifted her hand from the table and softly squeezed it reassuringly.

"It's OK, Kate. Just let it out. It's been buried away in there far too long. Imagine your tears are like a cool mountain waterfall. You are standing under the rushing water and it is cleansing away all of the darkness and forcing out the terrible sadness and undeserved self-loathing that you have hidden away in that secret tomb for such a long time. There are no coincidences in life and you are here with me today so that you can finally begin to heal. The next step is to find someone, a professional, to talk to so you can process what happened to you and try to extract something positive that will assist you today. Someone once told me, when I was in the midst of my very violent and ugly divorce that the best way to heal yourself is to reach out and heal another human being. I know it's hard to imagine that you could possibly help someone else feeling as broken as you do in this moment, but you *can* and you *need* to, for you. Use your story and your pain to suture the wounds of other women who have suffered the same kind of abuse."

A full hour had passed and Kate's treatment was over. She wiped the tears from her eyes. She pursed her lips together, inhaled the miraculous new clarity and illumined truth, filled her cheeks with still more tension and buried trauma, then blew out a forceful, liberating breath.

"Somehow I feel lighter and more hopeful than I can ever remember feeling," she confessed. "I guess I just needed to tell someone and let it out. Thank you!"

"You are most welcome and I thank you too for trusting me and allowing me to do what I do. This work is my bliss and I find it extremely fulfilling. Each time I use *my* life story to help someone else like you, I continue to heal myself as well. It's a continuous, extraordinary process. That's why we are all here anyway—to be of assistance to each other— spiritual partners on an earthly path. Whatever we give out to the world always comes back to us multiplied. You were a gift to me just as you see me as a gift to you. Amazing how it all works so perfectly."

"I HAVE LEARNED TO USE MORE
THAN MY FIVE PHYSICAL SENSES
IN BOTH MY WORK
AND MY PERSONAL LIFE.
BY WORKING
IN PARTNERSHIP WITH SPIRIT,
I AM ABLE TO SEE BEYOND
WHAT IS PRESENTED TO ME
AND EXPERIENCE MIRACLES—
SOMETHING POSSIBLE FOR US ALL."

# A Stroke of Inspiration

"**O**K," I interjected, unable to hide my irritation. "I apologize for interrupting, but you are the third person from Oceanic Spa that has called me about this woman, Lucy Miller! I have already been informed that she is a client who is very specific about what she wants in a treatment and that she requires deep tissue. I am also aware that the last therapist who treated her said Lucy stopped the massage in the beginning because it was not deep enough, abruptly got off the table and walked out. I realize that you don't really know my work, since I just started working for Oceanic but you have to trust me when I tell you I can handle her requests, and I can guarantee that she will be happy with her treatment."

I'm sure I sounded a bit cocky and overly self-assured. However, I have great confidence in my ability as a therapist and have never had anyone tell me I wasn't deep enough or that my work was not focused and effective. I realized that they were just trying to warn me, which I appreciated. At the same time they were trying to avoid another problem with Lucy being disappointed. I assured the worried employee that all would be fine and to please not have anyone else call me. Hanging up the phone I wondered how difficult Lucy had really been or if the staff was overexaggerating. I loved a challenge, however, so I was really looking forward to treating Lucy the following day.

As I viewed her chart moments before her arrival, I found that her problem was more than simply aching, sore muscles. Lucy had a stroke about five years prior to that day that left her with partial paralysis on the right side of her body. I wasn't sure how severe it was but I then realized that if she was not receiving focused work for this issue, I could completely understand her frustration.

It was midwinter and bitterly cold when I treated Lucy for the first time. She came into the spa wearing shorts, sneakers and a light denim jacket. She appeared to be about sixty years old. She was five feet two inches tall with shoulder length baby-fine blond hair with bangs that framed her angular face. She looked very German to me, with a strong athletic build. The first thing I noticed were her soft, expressive eyes that spoke volumes about the sadness, loss and adversity that she had been called to endure. Yet despite the evident pain, I could see a strength that was unmistakable. She held her head high and looked me straight in the eye.

"Hi Lucy, I'm Drusilla. How are you today?"

"I'll be better after the massage," she responded offering up her left hand, letting me realize that the spastic paralysis did not allow her any use of the right one. She added a skeptical "I hope," just to let me know she would be scrutinizing my every stroke.

"So, Lucy," I chimed right back as I led her down the hall toward the treatment room. "I hear you're a royal pain in the butt!"

Lucy stopped in her tracks, raised her left fist waist level and jabbed it defiantly onto her hip. I turned to face her and I saw a childish, mischievous sparkle in her eyes as she scanned my persona making her own quick assessment of me. Her stern countenance faded away and was replaced by a bright smile and a hearty laugh.

"Who the hell told you that," she demanded, thoroughly enjoying the fact that her reputation preceded her.

"Just about every receptionist who works at the spa," I said. "However, don't worry about a thing. You are in good hands, and I can guarantee you will not be disappointed."

We both laughed as I closed the door and allowed her to get ready for the massage. My perception had been correct. I sensed, as she walked into the spa, that this woman was like a dog that could smell fear. I intuitively surmised that she would appreciate someone who would challenge her. She covered up her fear and daily struggles with a bravado that was not really who she was. In actuality, what she wanted was a strong therapist and a healer who would give her hope, and a belief that she really could get well. I was determined to be that person.

That first time I treated Lucy was over four years ago. She was more than happy with my work. She continued to come to me every two weeks until recently when she moved to Florida to be with her children and grandchildren. She was a difficult treatment for me, taking a great deal of energy and effort, a whole lot of prayer, and spiritual healing. Lucy made some progress but it seemed to me that her limitations, unfortunately, might be permanent. Nevertheless, I tried to help her. I had to use most of my body weight just to pry open her hand so that I could stretch the muscles and allow them to relax. I worked to ease the tension in her left leg caused by her limited use of the right one. The work was intensely focused and left me feeling both gratified and exhausted at the same time.

Lucy was so grateful for how much I did for her, and she expressed it each and every time I saw her. Yet, over the years, it was Lucy who gave so much to me. We became fast friends. I was in awe of, and inspired by, her inner strength, her optimism, and her refusal to allow the adversities in her life to dampen her spirit or take away her joy. I learned that she too had endured a difficult marriage, from which she had escaped. She lived alone with severe disabilities and yet she did everything for herself. She drove, painted her house, shoveled snow, raked leaves, planted gardens, and worked full time as a home care nurse, all with the use of only one arm and limited mobility. God knows how she managed, but she did. She wanted no pity, and you really couldn't pity her. Like a cowboy in a rodeo, she took life by the horns, wrestled her adversity to the ground, and made it her friend.

Lucy made me laugh until I cried many times. She didn't take bull from anyone and didn't stop at anything if she wanted her way. She once told me a story about when she was in the hospital as a young woman because of a back problem. She felt she was better and wanted to go home but the doctors insisted on keeping her for another week. So for several days she collected sheets and on "liberation day" she called a friend and told her to park her car under the second floor window of her hospital room at a specific time. She tied the sheets together, secured them to the leg of her bed and climbed out. The hospital was not at all happy with her, but sure enough, Lucy got her way.

One day, after having known her for a few years, and immediately after having treated her, she asked me if I would do her a favor. Her hesitant tone and the shy, tentative way she asked led me to believe it was a huge favor.

"Of course," I said, without hesitation, wondering what in the world she could need from me.

"Do you think you could put my hair up into a ponytail? I always loved wearing my hair that way but since my stroke I can't do it for myself. It would mean so much to me if you could do it for me."

It was then that I realized how difficult it must be for her to do even the littlest things for herself. Yet, she never complained. My admiration, in that moment, rose to a new level as I began to brush her beautiful soft, baby-like hair and gently pull it up into the rubber band, securing it tightly, just the way she liked it. As I did, she let out a sigh and smiled like a little girl who just got her very first baby doll on Christmas morning. She wrapped her good arm around my neck and told me how much it meant to her. Every time I treated her after that, I put her hair into her favorite updo and each time she left me with two extraordinary gifts that I still hold close to my heart—her joyful, sincere gratitude and her beautiful, radiant smile. I miss her!

"IN SELFLESSLY GIVING TO OTHERS,
I ALWAYS RECEIVE
SO MUCH MORE IN RETURN,
IN WAYS I COULD NEVER
HAVE IMAGINED.
LUCY REAFFIRMED FOR ME
THAT I WILL NEVER GIVE UP,
NO MATTER WHAT THE ADVERSITY
OR HOW HOPELESS
A SITUATION MIGHT SEEM."

# *Luminescent Darkness*

*T*he day started in a most peaceful sort of way. I awoke to the beauty and tranquility of a sunny, late summer morning. As I sat outside among the fading and withering foliage, I felt oddly comforted. Trees were already beginning to alter their appearance as subtle hints of reds, yellows and oranges dotted their still mostly green attire. The lazy sun slept in a bit late these days, witnessed by the increasing hours of darkness. I gazed with anticipation toward the eastern sky awaiting the first glimpse of crimson that would blazon the beginning of a beautiful, new day.

"Interesting how joyful I feel," I mused. "Usually as the summer is about to bid farewell, I feel a mild sadness and a desperate desire to hold back time so that I can enjoy this season of warmth, vitality, and incredible color just a little while longer. I guess I should just enjoy the moment and bask in these wonderful feelings of serenity."

And so I did, settling into the magical presence of "the now," while sipping my hot coffee and breathing in the fragrant aroma of hazelnut that wafted through the crisp, moist air. Bunnies, squirrels, and chipmunks hopped and scurried through the slightly overgrown grass in search of their morning meal. All was well and complete in my world, and I savored every moment.

Somewhere around midmorning, I suppose, there was a shift. Anxiety, uneasiness, and restlessness began to settle deep into the core of my solar plexus. It was puzzling as there was no clear reason for the abrupt transformation. It wasn't accompanied by any defining thoughts that might have shaped and sculpted this mysterious, unsettling mood.

I arrived at work breathing deeply, in an attempt to will myself back to the peacefulness of the early dawn. It didn't work. I sat quietly in my treatment room waiting for my client to arrive and I prayed.

"Dear God, I need to be there fully for the person I am about to treat. Please, even for just a moment, help me to rise above my own emotions and feelings; take away this anxiety so that I can be of service," I pleaded.

"Dru, your client is here," announced the receptionist, Liz, quickly pulling me out of my moment of solitude and prayer.

I walked to the lobby and greeted Pamela, a woman who appeared to be about seventy-five years of age.

"Hello, Pam. I'm Drusilla. Please follow me," I instructed mustering up a smile that was forced, shaky and unnatural. "How are you Pam," I queried, as we approached the massage room.

"Stress, so much stress," she uttered almost inaudibly shaking her head from side-to-side as she shuffled down the hallway.

Her head hung forward, her gaze was fixated on the floor almost as if the weight of her worries made it impossible to lift it. Her voice was raspy, deep and gruff, and her abrupt response was followed by several crackly coughs indicating a likelihood that she had been smoking for quite some time.

"OK, maybe you'd like to talk about it," I offered. "I'll be back in a few moments after you have disrobed and are comfortably on the table … start face up, please."

"Do you think talking about what's bothering you would help," I asked as I began the treatment by gently massaging her forehead and temples.

"It's been forty years, you know, forty years. All that stuff—I just don't know how I can face it—and him, I'm so angry at him for dying and leaving me with all these problems," she rambled, as I tried to piece together what she was trying to tell me.

"Forty years of what?" I asked.

"Living in that house, being married to him, raising our children, all the memories, all the stuff—now I have to sell the house. What do I do with all the memories? Do I throw them away? Every time I try to clean out a space, I find pictures of our life together, things he gave me—just so many memories and I fall apart over and over again. I can't get through this."

Her voice began to crack as tears pooled in her sad, tired eyes. She reached up to wipe them away and then grabbed her head in both hands in what seemed to be an attempt to stop the endless stream of worries, visions of the past, fears of the future, and an unrelenting pain over how life had picked her up, swung her around, and hurled her into a place she no longer recognized and desperately wanted to escape from. I reached down and took her hand in mine.

"You know Pam, even though you are in terrible pain right now, and feeling lost and afraid, there is something you can do that can ease your sadness. Somehow, even though it may not seem possible for you right now, if you take some time to just step away from your own stuff and reach out to someone else who is also hurting, you begin to heal. A very wise man told me this when I was going through the darkest time in my life. I tried it and it worked."

"Hmmm," she reflected. "You know, now that you say that, the only time I feel good lately is when I bring food over to an elderly friend of mine who has cancer. She is so grateful just to have my company and for just a moment I feel happy and I forget my pain."

"That's the key," I sang out, overjoyed that she understood. "Being of service to others in times of need has a way of making us feel stronger and gives us hope that we can handle what life gives us, no matter how difficult."

"Yes," she quickly interjected as her mood lightened and her energy brightened. "Today I saw a medivan and I thought about the person inside and how they were probably ill or injured. Maybe they couldn't walk; maybe they were dying. So I said to myself, 'Pam, you put your big girl pants on, put a smile on your face and be thankful. Things could be worse.'"

"So you see Pam," I assured her. "You know instinctively what you need to do to get through this time and to heal. You are still here on this earth because there are people who need your love, friendship, and wisdom, and you need theirs."

Pam's energy became almost childlike and I could sense her despair transform into abundant hope. The worn crevices in her face and the deep lines around her eyes that had been crying tears of grief, loss and sorrow were suddenly filled with an invisible, perceptible light. She looked younger, happier, and at peace.

The treatment was over. She thanked me for the gift I had given her. She left and as she was walking out the door, I felt overwhelming gratitude. I realized that a miracle had occurred, and she had unknowingly given me a precious gift as well. She allowed me to do exactly what I was trying to teach her to do. I rose above my own anxiety and pain, reached out to another soul who needed me and miraculously my anxiety was gone. Healing was my reward for "being of service."

"WHENEVER I FEEL
AS IF I HAVE NOTHING TO GIVE,
A GOLDEN HUMAN ANGEL,
WHO NEEDS ME,
APPEARS TO HELP ME REMEMBER,
ONCE AGAIN, THAT
THE GREATEST MEDICINE
FOR OUR PAIN AND SUFFERING
IS TO BE OF SERVICE TO OTHERS."

# *Loose Ends*
## *(A story of heartache, enlightenment, and hope)*

*I*t's midafternoon by the water's edge on an unusually warm June day. Gazing out upon the expanse of azure blue sea and turquoise blue sky, there appears to be no clear line separating the two. The hues deepen and lighten for reasons she is unaware of. Listening to the waves as they gently release their consistent swell onto the rocky, northern shore of Long Island, she feels nurtured and comforted. The only other sounds are the distant drone of a boat engine, the muffled squeal of a gliding gull, and the silent music of sailboats. The fragrant spring breeze blows softly through their regal masts, allowing them to float easily and slowly on the calm, tranquil sea. Her attention is drawn to a tiny loon that dips down beneath the surface in search of food. More than thirty seconds go by before he pops back up some ten feet or so, due west. He continues this maritime dance and she is lulled even further into an altered stated of consciousness. Just as easily as she was drawn to the loon, her eyes then move closer to the shore as she sees two horseshoe crabs, gliding side by side, patrolling the water's edge like two military tanks, ready to take advantage of any tasty morsels brought in by the incoming tide. All of these sights, sounds and smells have finally allowed her to find the peace that has eluded her for the last few days.

Only hours ago, she teetered on the edge of a serious emotional meltdown. The events of the last week, with her nineteen-year-old daughter, have left her with a depression, the likes of which she has never known. Slipping back into her pattern of abuse and irrational thought, her daughter tears open, once again, the gaping, painful wound that had slowly and gratefully healed over the time she was away at college….

A week has passed now since the manic episode when her daughter, Amanda, hit her. Her child's response to having lost control is outrageous. Fear, utter and complete fear, is her irrational motivation for the incomprehensible aftershock. Amanda is intensely afraid of her inability to control her moods. She is terrified of becoming the illness that she fights against every moment and has fought against since she was a very small child. Knowing her mother's lingering issues of abandonment and neglect, she has a perfect solution. There will be no apology, no reaching out to make amends. Instead, she will bully her mom with silence interspersed with hateful glares, pulling back her love and hoping her mom will feel a sense of loss that will make her vulnerable. Amanda's goal is that her mother will reach out to her in a way that either levels the blame field, or, better yet, has her being the victim, and her mother the neglectful, inadequate mom….

Almost another week has gone by. Amanda continues her harsh and cruel stance. She goes to and from work and out with friends without a word. She is angry that Jason, her stepfather, and her mom, Tanya, gave her an ultimatum; if she raises her hand to her mother again, they will call the police and she will be removed from the house. Tanya is grateful for Jason's support and she is resolved that, despite the fact that Amanda is her daughter, she will not be abused or victimized ever again. She knows her daughter and is sure that Amanda is frightened that she may not be able to control herself and will be taken away from her mom. You would think if she loved her mother so much and was fearful of not having her in her life, she would not hurt her. That is the illness … not the lovely, caring, compassionate, sweet, loving soul who is her cherished, beautiful child. There are two different Amandas. Her daughter's ability to be loving and peaceful as opposed to manic, abusive, and violent is dependent upon a delicate balance of chemicals in her brain. Professionals have labeled it bipolar or borderline personality disorder. As a young teen she pleaded with Tanya to allow her to try to get better without medication. She worked hard and did get much better. The joyful Amanda is in control most of the time. However, as evidenced by this latest regression, intense stress is a likely trigger that spirals her back out of control and into that dark and frightening space. Once there, she loses her essential self, blacks out, and leaps from that precarious cliff representing sanity, out into a bottomless expanse of insanity, pain, and violence—and her mom is her only target—her safe place. She knows Tanya will never abandon her and will always love her, so it is there that she releases all of her anxiety, anger, and confusion.

Yesterday Tanya awoke to a dark, viscous, palpable cloud of acute sadness hanging over her. She felt crushed by its weight and intensity. She found herself feeling hopeless and lost. She couldn't fix this. She couldn't help her daughter. She found herself drowning in a sea of self-loathing and self-doubt. She spent the day almost catatonic as she was rendered incapacitated by a relentless, boring ache in her heart.

"A mother's love should be enough," she agonized. "I could have done something more to help her—more counseling, more encouragement, more perfect mothering."

Then in response to her anguished prayers she received a gift. Her older sister, Dawn, wrote her an email. Somehow, she seemed to know Tanya needed her. Normally Tanya doesn't lean on anyone in times of difficulty, except her husband, of course. She feels it's not fair to burden someone when there is no solution. It only makes the other person feel helpless. She normally works through the adversity, finds the lesson, and then shares what she learned. For some reason, though, this time she did lean on her sister. They exchanged emails back and forth, and Dawn tried to remind Tanya of how special she is and that it isn't her fault. Tears flowed the entire day from an endless well of torment but were transformed into gratitude as she allowed her big sister to comfort her. In the last email she received from Dawn she told Tanya that she was about to say a rosary for her and for Amanda. Her sister has said the rosary three times a day her entire life, so Tanya figured she must have one special place in heaven and lots of clout. She was grateful.

The following morning Tanya awoke with the most amazing sense of peace and inner tranquility. It was baffling because nothing had really changed. Sitting outside on the back patio with her morning coffee, reveling in the soft crystals of sunlight that began filtering through the newly formed, lush, green canopy, she prayed trying to understand this sudden shift. As clear as day, words flowed into her mind, so audibly that she was certain they came from a place outside of her.

*"It was your sister's fervent and heartfelt prayer for you. Though the answer to this crisis, as of yet, is not clear, her prayer restored your sense of peace, lifted from you the heaviness and sadness, and brought you back to the awareness and blessedness of your beautiful soul. Always remember, in the end, the only opinion of you that matters is your own. Self-love and self-acceptance are the foundation, the rich soil from which the delicate flowers of inner peace and true happiness bloom. So, bloom where God has planted you! You are exactly where you are supposed to be right now. Remember who you have always been and how pure your intentions are always. So much good has come from those intentions and they far outweigh the times when you may have fallen short. You are loved by God eternally. However, in order to be able to really feel the impact and*

*intensity of that love you must always love and honor yourself."*

Several years have gone by. There is no complete conclusion to this story as both Tanya and Amanda are growing and evolving. Amanda is now twenty-three years old, has worked hard at believing in and loving herself, and she is becoming a beautiful, mature young woman. The turmoil of her past seems to be receding as she truly owns her magnificence and radiates her inner beauty. Tanya continues to believe in Amanda and in their relationship. Most importantly, however, she believes in herself! She has come to understand that, in order for people in our lives to honor and cherish us, including our children, we must first honor and cherish ourselves. Guilt and shame serve no useful purpose in good parenting. Self-love and self-respect are far greater teachers. She cannot control others' behavior. She can, however, keep herself healthy and joyful no matter what the circumstances in her life. She is determined to choose positive thoughts and let any negative ones attempting entry to float softly into the heavens. There, she is confident they will be transformed and returned to her in the form of inspiration, enlightenment, and hope. She will choose self-love. She will offer to Amanda unconditional love along with clear personal boundaries and will offer her honest consistent, open lines of communication. They have both promised each other to focus on the good in their relationship and they believe that, as a result, the good will continue to grow.

"UNCONDITIONAL SELF-LOVE
IS THE FOUNDATION UPON WHICH
A LIFE OF PEACE IS BUILT.
I WILL NOT ALLOW
ANY CIRCUMSTANCE OR PERSON
TO DISTURB OR TAKE AWAY
MY PRECIOUS SENSE OF SELF-WORTH.
THE ONLY OPINION OF ME
THAT REALLY MATTERS IS MY OWN."

# *Having Hope Leads to Joy*

*J*essica dropped the phone. Throwing her head back fiercely against the wall in an unconscious attempt to dull and deflect the pain in her heart, she crumpled to the floor and balled herself into a fetal position. Her husband, Ron sat down next to her.

"I'm sorry Jess. I feel so helpless," Ron comforted, wrapping both arms around her. "We can try again as soon as the doctor says it's OK."

Nothing Ron could say could stop the pain. How he wished he could curtail the torrent of tears that was creating a direct, perverse union between her tortured mind and that raw, emotional space in her gut. Feelings of hopelessness combined with intense grief and a profound, unrelenting sorrow created an inferno of blazing hurt deep in her belly. He couldn't stop any of it. All he could offer was his tremendous love for his wife. So he pulled her closer. He needed to be her rock, her strength, her faith, and her hope. The truth was, though, that the devastating news confirming that the in-vitro fertilization had failed once again shattered his heart as well.

"We have to have faith, Jess. We have to believe that one day we will have a family. We'll keep trying and if the in-vitro doesn't work, we'll adopt. Think of all of the beautiful little babies all over the world that are just waiting for couples just like us to love them."

Jess lifted her head and turned to Ron looking deeply and inquisitively into his eyes.

"But you said you didn't want to adopt," she sniffed narrowing her eyes as she tried to discern his level of honesty. "What changed your mind?"

"I'm not sure exactly," Ron responded. "I love you. I love us. I guess

I allowed myself to really envision being a father. I want that. I want us to be family and I believe everything happens for a reason. Maybe we are going through all of this because there is a little baby, a soul who is supposed to be with us. Maybe he or she is just waiting for us because it is destined. I'm not saying we should give up on having a child of our own because I know how important it is for you to be pregnant. But if it doesn't happen, then we'll adopt, but one way or another we will have our family, I promise."

Jess unfurled her arms from around her legs and threw them around Ron's neck. She never loved him more than she did at that moment. She knew with absolute certainty that he didn't just love her, but he cherished her, embracing all the good, accepting with patience and understanding all of her faults and insecurities. He was her partner, and the best friend she had ever had. She trusted him with her heart especially now when it was so delicate and fragile.

The next two attempts at in-vitro were unsuccessful so Ron and Jess decided to pursue adoption. After gathering enough paperwork and information to fill every bit of counter space in their home, they finally decided that they would adopt a child from Vietnam.

It was the beginning of September in 2001 when all of the appropriate documents had been filed, and they made their plans to go to Vietnam and bring home a little baby girl. They were both nervous for many reasons but made up their minds that they would not focus on all of the things that could or might go wrong. Instead they would think only about that moment when they would hold their little girl in their arms.

Then came 9/11 and their adoption plans went into a precarious place of uncertainty. Jess and Ron had no idea how this horrible event would affect their dream of meeting their baby daughter. Even Jess's baby shower that was planned for the Saturday after 9/11 was doubtful.

"Ron, how can we celebrate when so many people are suffering and in pain? Will anyone even want to come, and is it even right that we ask them to?"

Their families convinced them that everyone needed a happy occasion so they went forward with the shower. Everyone did come—a true testament to how much their family and friends loved them. As a way of acknowledging what a sad time in our history this was for everyone, Ron and Jess decided to do something thoughtful to help everyone forget for just a moment, the horror of the last week. On a table, by the front door was a box and next to it pieces of paper and pencils. Their guests were asked to take a minute before entering and write down all of their worries or concerns and leave them in the box. They were free to take them back when they left or leave them and ask God to help heal their broken hearts. No one took their worries with them, but instead left them in God's hands.

The departure date for Ron and Jess to go to Vietnam to finalize the adoption was pushed ahead a month but they finally did leave at the beginning of December.

"Ron, we've been here in Vietnam now for three weeks," Jess announced with frustration. "They told us it would only take a week, ten days at the most. I'm scared that we will never be allowed to take our baby girl home. I don't understand why they wouldn't be more eager to just get it done. Did you see all of those women in the streets trying to sell their babies? It's awful. What will happen to them and how could a mother just sell her child to a complete stranger?"

"I guess they must be pretty desperate," Ron replied. "But we can't worry about all of those children right now, only our own. Just don't lose hope, Jess. We've come this far and we're not going home without our baby."

A whole month went by. Jess and Ron had left for Vietnam on December 6th and were supposed to be home for Christmas. The holidays came and went, and their families' Christmas trees stayed up, fully decorated into January with all the unwrapped presents underneath waiting for Jess, Ron and baby to come home. Finally, on January 10, 2002, they set foot back onto American soil with their beautiful baby girl. They raced home as quickly as they could to introduce her to Jess's parents.

"Mom, Dad," announced Jess excitedly. "We would like you to meet your granddaughter. Her name is 'Hope' because that is what it took for us to keep believing through all of the setbacks and disappointments that we would finally have our family. So here she is … our little miracle, Hope!"

Jess's mom, Joan, gazed in awe at Jessica, her lovely daughter. She was so proud of the incredible young woman she had become. It had been hard on her as well, seeing her own little girl struggle as she fought courageously to make her dream of motherhood a reality.

"Can I hold her," Joan pleaded anxiously.

Jess nodded with a radiant smile and her mom scooped little Hope into her arms as tears of joy fell softly onto the silky smooth skin of her beautiful granddaughter.

"We have another surprise too," continued Ron. "We got a call from the adoption agency on our way home. Today Hope's biological mother gave birth to another baby girl, Hope's sister. They wanted to know if we would like to adopt her as well. We told them, absolutely yes!"

Six months later Jess and Ron traveled, once again, to Vietnam and brought home a second gorgeous little girl. They called her "Joy." Their family is no longer a distant dream but a magnificent reality born from the fertile seeds of love, *Hope,* faith and *Joy!*

"LIFE DOESN'T ALWAYS
TURN OUT THE WAY WE PLANNED.
SOMETIMES, BEYOND THE PAIN
OF HEARTACHE, GRIEF, AND LOSS,
AWAITS AN EVEN MORE
MIRACULOUS GIFT
JUST WAITING TO BE RECEIVED.
WE ALWAYS NEED HOPE
SO THAT WE CAN FIND OUR JOY."

# *Torrents of Prayers*

"*I* wonder what could be keeping Kristina," I questioned out loud as Sam and I sat in the bistro room having our morning coffee. I know she is only five minutes late but she is always so prompt I could set my clock by her. It sounds crazy but I have this awful feeling that something is terribly wrong."

I waited nervously. Kristina never arrived at our house that morning for her regular weekly massage. After about an hour had gone by, I called. The phone rang several times and I thought it was going to the answering machine, when suddenly she answered. By the sound of her voice, I quickly realized that she was crying.

"Kristina, it's Dru, "Are you OK," I asked.

"I have cancer," she wept. "The doctor told me it's inflammatory breast cancer (IBC). I have an appointment at Sloan Kettering Cancer Hospital in NYC. When I got home, I looked it up online. It's very rare and really aggressive. The survival rate is not good. I just found out yesterday and I'm not handling it too well. I can't stop crying. I just can't believe this is happening to me. I don't understand why. Oh, I'm so sorry about this morning. I just forgot."

I was stunned. Kristina was a young woman about thirty-seven years of age. She was vibrant, healthy, and worked out on a regular basis. At the time, she had a ten-year-old daughter named Lauren. She was a very content stay-at-home mom and the wife of a successful real estate broker. She had been referred to me by an old client that I had treated when I had my massage business on the South Shore of Long Island. Kris and I hit it off immediately. I loved her dry wit, her sense of humor and her genuine, honest sensitivity. She was feisty and strong and had no trouble speaking her mind and letting you know if she thought you were out of line. I had been treating her for a few years, and I looked forward, every week, to our hour-long sessions when we laughed, sometimes cried, and always completely enjoyed each other's company.

"Oh, Kris," I responded. "I'm so sorry. Please don't worry one bit about this morning. Is there anything I can do for you? You know I am here for you if you need me, even if you just need to talk."

"Thanks, Dru," she sobbed making it very difficult to understand her. "I don't know what my future's gonna be right now, so I don't know when I'll be able to come again. I'll let you know as soon as I do."

"You just concentrate on getting well, and again, if you need me I'm only a phone call away."

I hung up the phone feeling absolutely shocked. I pressed the palms of my hands against my temples trying to wrap my mind around what I had just heard. I was aware that every day more and more women are diagnosed with breast cancer. However, that fact didn't make the news any less devastating. This was personal. I cared about Kristina. She had become part of my life each and every week for several years. I began to envision the painful, unavoidable ordeal she would be facing in her battle against this deadly disease, and I ached for her and for her family.

"God," I thought, "How I wish there was something I could have said in that moment to help ease her pain. If only I had a magic wand that I could wave ceremoniously over her diseased breast and heal it; abracadabra, no more cancer."

I felt so helpless and of course, the only weapon I had at my disposal was prayer. So, in that moment and for many more over the next several months, I prayed and prayed and prayed. I didn't hear from Kristina at all during that time, and I struggled over whether I should call. She felt much more like a friend than merely a client. However, we did not socialize beyond my treatment room so I thought I should respect her privacy and hoped that she would call me.

I ran into her in the grocery store a few months later with her daughter. She looked tired and spent and was wearing a red bandana on her head hinting that her hair had fallen out from bouts of chemotherapy. We exchanged pleasantries and I asked her how she was doing. She responded with very few words saying she was OK and was looking forward to the chemo being over soon. She told me that with IBC they needed to start chemotherapy immediately, get the cancer controlled, and then do the mastectomy. From what she understood, this was the opposite procedure from more common forms of breast cancer when the mastectomy is done first. I told her that she was in my heart and my prayers. We hugged and said goodbye.

A few weeks later Kristina called. She was excited that the chemo was finished, and the surgery to remove her breast was scheduled. She was anxious to get back to her weekly massage routine and reclaim her life. I was so relieved and happy for her. She began coming again, and over the next several weeks her hair started to grow back. She gained more and more strength and stamina, now that all the chemicals were no longer coursing through her body. Everything seemed to be working out, and Kristina was on her way back to health.

Unfortunately, I was wrong! Shortly thereafter, I received an email from her. She sounded even more distraught than when she first received the news about her cancer.

"Dru," she wrote. "They found lesions on my liver. They cancelled the surgery. It doesn't look good. What will my little girl do without me? I can't leave her. She needs me. Oh my God, I have never felt more alone or felt such terrible sadness in my whole life. I'm so scared and I feel beaten down and just plain hopeless."

"OK, Kris," I responded immediately feeling completely devastated and shaken to the core but doing my best not to show it. "Don't you give up! I truly believe in the power of prayer and I am going to engage every prayer warrior I know right now. The only thing you need to do is believe."

I hung up the phone and within minutes sent a copy of her email to everyone I knew.

"Dear prayer warriors," I wrote. "Please stop whatever you are doing and pray. Please don't wait a minute, an hour, or a day … please, please pray for Kristina right now. She needs a miracle, and I know we can make one happen for her."

Within minutes the responses began flowing into my inbox and I forwarded them on to Kristina to help give her hope and faith ("Prayers coming now … Praying like a torrential rainstorm … God bless Kristina and send angels to heal her.") The emails kept coming one after another. I could feel the intensity, ferocity and faith behind every word they wrote.

After a couple of weeks I received a call from Kristina.

"Dru, you aren't going to believe this. They did a CAT scan and all the doctors at Sloan Kettering had a big meeting about the results. It seems the tumors on my liver—all of them—are shrinking. They told me they are baffled. The exact words they said were, 'Cancer doesn't behave like this.' They told me I had my miracle. It was an amazing moment."

My tears of joy and elation were as abundant as the many prayers that had been offered for my dear friend. That was over four years ago. Kristina still lives with some fear each time she has another test, worried that the cancer may return. However, with each positive result she becomes more confident that she will live to see her little girl graduate from college, get married, and have babies of her own. She has a newfound appreciation for her life, and has learned to nurture and care for herself more. Through much counseling and inner work, she now sees the gift that was buried deep in the center of that pain and adversity called IBC. It taught her to truly love, accept, and appreciate herself in ways she has never done before.

I am so grateful to have Kristina in my life today. I believe, in part at least, that I owe it to the incredible power of love and prayer from not only people who knew and loved her but from complete loving strangers as well. I continue to engage and appreciate all of my trusted prayer warriors who are always ever ready to step up and make more miracles happen.

"AT TIMES, WHEN I FEEL THE MOST HELPLESS AMIDST LIFE'S TRIALS AND CHALLENGES, IF I PAUSE AND TURN MY HEART AND MIND TO GOD AND BELIEVE THAT A MIRACLE IS POSSIBLE, I RECAPTURE HOPE. THE OUTCOME MAY NOT ALWAYS BE WHAT I PRAYED FOR BUT I CAN USUALLY, IN THE END, SEE AND APPRECIATE THE GIFT, THE BLESSING, AND THE TREASURE OF THE SOUL."

# *Body Secrets*

*I*t had been a very tough day, a lot of deep tissue massage. It was also one of those days when clients told me their painful stories and where I could clearly feel traumas that had burrowed their way deep inside the bellies of muscles. These kinds of days are deeply gratifying but can also be very draining if I'm not careful to protect myself energetically. I thought I had, but I was beginning to run out of steam.

As I changed the linen on the massage table and prepared for my next and final massage of the day, I said my usual prayer: "God, please allow me to be a vehicle for healing and light. My hands are your hands." I walked down the hallway leading to the waiting room that was dimly lit with candles and aromatherapy scents. I breathed in deeply and shook my hands trying to release any leftover energy from the previous client.

"The owner sure has a flair for decorating and creating a peaceful and tranquil setting," I mused. "No wonder she is always so busy in this place."

I opened the door to the waiting area and called for my next client, "Martin Hampton?"

"Yes, that's me," a voice called from the corner of the room. A tall, cheerful man jumped up and quickly walked toward me. Marty seemed to be in his mid-forties and was slim and quite attractive.

"Hi, I'm Drusilla, and I will be your therapist today."

"Nice to meet you, Drusilla," he said as he extended his right hand in front of him. He shook my hand so firmly, I cringed in pain. I have learned that many times clients will squeeze my hand tightly to see if I am strong enough to give them a good deep treatment. He was one of them.

Martin was about six feet tall with very expressive but somewhat sad-looking, almond-shaped, brown eyes. His hair was a light auburn, short with a longer piece in the back that curled up slightly. It was winter and he was wearing a black peacoat with a grey scarf and grey gloves. I could tell that fashion was of utmost importance to him, and he could really pull it off.

As we walked down the hallway towards the treatment room I asked, "How are you today?" With that he started talking nonstop about anything and everything. His speech was so rapid and choppy that I had a hard time keeping up with him. He reeked of anxiety. It was strange since, initially his appearance gave the indication of a very calm self-assured man.

"Uh oh," I thought. I'd been doing this work for long enough to know that something was very wrong with his energy. I got a strong sense that this was going to be an intense session—a lot more than just tissue manipulation.

After he disrobed and got comfortably on the table, I knocked on the door and entered. Having consulted with my guides, I was quite sure that he had been directed to my treatment room by his own spiritual guidance for a reason other than massage, even though he was completely unaware of it. When I walked in he immediately began filling up the silence with his incessant chatter. When he paused to take a breath, I took advantage of the moment and told him a few things about the kind of work I do. I informed him that I could read his energy by focusing on his chakras (energy vortexes down the midline of the body) using a pendulum. I asked him if he would like me to do that. He was intrigued, open, and immediately agreed.

I began with the 6th chakra which is the area on the forehead between the eyes. It is the intuitive center where we receive guidance from our higher self or soul. I held the pendulum over it and it began to spin.

"This energy is sluggish and appears to be opening and closing, indicating that although you do hear the still small voice of your soul at times, you don't trust that this wisdom is real, and you tighten the energy and stop receiving."

When I put the pendulum over the 5th or throat chakra it barely moved. A clear message came through, and I delivered it. "You are keeping a huge secret from someone very close to you in your life and it is causing this energy to nearly shut down."

"No good," I thought. I could tell I was heading towards something pretty big.

"The heart chakra is also sluggish and tight. It feels as if there is a lot of confusion about some significant relationships in your life. There is also a veil of protective energy around it." As I explained what I was sensing, I could see a single tear in the corner of one eye, but he said nothing.

The first and second chakras, one located in the pubic area and the other slightly above it, were spinning out of control. He was losing a lot of energy from these two centers. "OK, I'm just gonna say this. You are misdirecting your sexual energy somewhere it doesn't belong, which I imagine is related to the secret you are keeping and the confusion in your heart. I suspect that you are having some pain in the lower part of your body as well. You need to understand, Martin, that you can't keep secrets from the body. If you misuse energy in this way it can and many times does cause illness."

Marty now had a very, sad remorseful look on his face and he proceeded to tell me his story. He was married and had been having an affair for over ten years. He related that he wasn't sure if he loved either woman, but he also said that he was very fond of his wife and that she was a wonderful woman. He was afraid of committing to either, so he divided his love between the two of them to keep himself safe, and protected from being hurt. He was neither happy nor unhappy in his marriage because he never gave it a chance. He also confirmed that he was indeed having some physical pain in that area.

"Martin, you can't keep going down this path. If you do, you will never experience what a fulfilling relationship is and you may, very well, jeopardize your health. You need to choose, not just for yourself but for those two women." Tearfully he nodded. I knew he had a lot of soul searching to do, and I knew I needed to add him to my list of people to pray for. I told so many people I would pray for them, over the years, that I couldn't remember them all. So, I recorded them in a book and assumed God knew who was in there.

He left that day, and I didn't see him again for two years. He came in for a massage and while there, he told me the ending to the story. Shortly after I treated him the first time, he was diagnosed with a serious health issue. At that point he chose to end the affair and focus on his relationship with his wife. The more he let go, trusted and allowed himself to be vulnerable the more he fell in love with her. The health issue disappeared he said he was truly happy for the first time in his life.

"My life changed forever the day that you treated me," he offered, "and I just needed to thank you. I'm sorry it has taken me so long."

I graciously accepted his gratitude but quickly pointed out that I am only the vehicle and messenger. There is a power far greater than I who orchestrated the crossing of our paths and the eventual healing. I bowed my head and said a silent prayer feeling humbled and grateful to have been of service.

"THERE ARE NO SECRETS WITH
THE UNIVERSAL MIND OF GOD,
AND MISDIRECTED ENERGY
WILL FIND A WAY TO MANIFEST.
THE LAW OF KARMA
(CAUSE AND EFFECT)
IS ALWAYS ENGAGED
AND IN MOTION."

# Moving On and More ...

# Introduction to Moving On and More ...

So, my new friends, this is the beginning of the last section of *Treasures of the Soul*. However, there really is no true end because I still inhabit the amazing physical expression of my soul, my human body. My life here on the earth plane will continue for as long as this remains so, and I will continue to learn, teach, and evolve. I will continue to use the same process which I have shown you here, so that I can understand my life experiences and the information Spirit is trying to bring forth to me, and to all of us. I hope I have inspired you to do the same. As I mentioned in the beginning of the book, I would love to hear from you all. Tell me your stories. Yet, what is as equally important as recanting the experiences is for you to let me know how you have emerged from your adversities, how you have grown, and what you have learned as a result of them. I ask you to share with me and the world, your love, wisdom, and enlightenment so that we might remember a little more of our own strength, beauty, and magnificence. With your permission, of course, I will honor you by adding your story and your message to my next books, so we can all continue to be a unifying force for goodness and light. You will find my website and my email address at the end of the book.

This section is far longer than the others I suppose, because I am writing about my life all the time now, rather than going back into my past and remembering what I believed to be significant memories from my earlier years. I have learned through my daily journaling that there are no memories or experiences more significant than others, even if they seem to be. There aren't any coincidences, as I have mentioned over and over. The smallest most insignificant moment can be life changing if we stay in the moment. We need to stay conscious and understand that each person and experience is there for a reason, has purpose, and can offer us a profound opportunity to learn, to teach, and to remember our divine self.

Moving On and More … contains stories from the time period when my marriage to Jake was finally over, and I had received full custody of Jake Asher, Brianne, and Allison. It continues on from there describing how my life changed when I met my current husband Sam, and when my dad and then estranged ex-father-in-law passed away. There are stories of my children and how they have grown up and moved on as well. Some are uplifting and inspirational, and some are acutely sad. Yet, again, the process of telling, then attempting to understand my experiences and uncover the message or lesson, is the same. There are still some unfinished stories being played out in the theatre of my life. These unfinished tales require me to embrace my faith and believe that all happens for a reason, and eventually I will understand the larger picture and uncover the divine design for it all.

So I thank you for sharing my journey with me. Thank you for allowing me to have a small place in your life. I hope that my life and my work have touched you in a way that will, indeed, inspire you to share your life and stories with me and many others who are fellow travelers on a spiritual path.

> **"I WISH FOR YOU ALL MUCH LOVE, LIGHT, AND LAUGHTER!"**

# *Buried Treasure*

*J*t was midsummer and the year was 2001. Sam and I had been in a committed relationship for almost a year. When my kids were with their dad on weekends, I usually spent time at Sam's house. On an early summer morning, we decided to take a ride to a harbor on the North Shore of Long Island to enjoy the sweetness of a beautiful, clear, sunny day as it began unfolding. The water had the appearance of being calm and tranquil like a still, slumbering child who dances and plays beneath the illusion of unconsciousness. I could feel the magical energy and life just below the surface, though it remained hidden from my physical eyes. My otherworldly senses suddenly came alive, and I could see with my mind's eyes all the vibrant life that a moment ago was invisible to me. I intuitively sensed the movement and the vibration, and it gave me a surge of energy and a feeling of joy that was a perfect accompaniment to the precious moment at hand. Having grown up near the bay and the ocean, I became sensitive to, and enamored by, the beauty and mystery of places such as this. I was at peace.

The sun hung lazily in the eastern sky, still reluctant to release the magnificent hues of orange and red that ushered in the beginning of a new day. Sam and I sat with our feet dangling over the edge of the dock. As we basked in the beauty of the moment, two regal and elegant swans glided aimlessly across the mirrored surface of infinity. There was an audible silence as we enjoyed the incredible connectedness and felt intense gratitude for our new and treasured love. Words served no useful purpose as we spoke to each other in a swirling dance of energy that moved back and forth, and in and out of our hearts. We breathed in the rainbow of luminescent colors that surrounded us, the turquoise blue of the water, pale blue of the sky, and the emerald green of the trees that stood like sentinels around the perimeter of the water's edge. The golden yellow blaze of the giant orb gave brilliance, light, and life to everything it touched. With each exhalation we slipped more profoundly into perfect unity with each other.

Sam reached over and grabbed my hand squeezing it gently, speaking volumes with his touch, and communicating far more with his heart than mere words could ever convey. I wondered if God gave us invaluable moments, such as these, so we could receive just a small glimpse of His immense, immeasurable Divine love for us. It made me want to hold fast to this gift and dive more deeply into the gently moving waters of heaven's passionate core.

I turned to Sam and as I looked into his kind, expressive, beautiful blue eyes, a wave of intense, uncontrollable, emotions rose spontaneously and without warning to the surface of my being. Tears welled in my eyes like a storm surge during one of Mother Nature's unpredictable tantrums. We were both taken by surprise.

"Are you OK?" he softly inquired, searching his mind for any possible explanation for my sudden shift.

"Yes ... no ... I don't know."

There were no thoughts that accompanied the painful feelings, the "pain body" that had come alive inside of me.

"Can you, please, just give me a few minutes to meditate and try to find the answer? Hopefully, I will, and then I will share it with you."

I had learned over the years that all the answers to my questions reside within me. I needed to go there so I did not misinterpret the confusing feelings that had surfaced unexpectedly. Sam nodded with acceptance, turning his gaze back toward the water and allowing me to move into my own private space so I could try to decipher the bewildering flood of hurt, pain, and anguish that did not fit the moment at all. The contrast was similar to a warm summer sun and blue sky that spewed forth cold white crystals of powdery, white snow. After a few pensive moments, I turned to him.

"It's you," I blurted out. "You and this place, together."

I could see the confusion in his eyes as I continued.

"My life before you, my marriage, the pain, the fear, the darkness … I buried it safely away in a small hidden space within me so that I could survive the trauma. All that had happened to me over those many years was locked away inside of me. I kept it buried, fearing that if I released its contents, I would be consumed and swallowed up by all of the heartache and sadness. Then I met you, the most beautiful, gentle, honest, and soulful person I have ever known. You helped me to trust again. You allowed me to believe in a fairy tale kind of love. You looked deeply inside my soul; you embraced it and cherished it in a way I didn't know was possible. I felt loved unconditionally. This amazing place is reflecting back to me the tremendous beauty that I see inside of you. You and this place are so much in contrast to the remaining darkness, and pain still locked away in my secret prison, that in this moment of intense polarity, the lock was blasted away, and the door flew open. It felt like I was finally able to let it all go—at least most of it." I hoped so, though I sensed there was yet more that I needed to face and release. "There is too much beauty, love and light in my life right now and it seeks to inhabit all the spaces and places inside of me, even the frightening cavern where I buried my painful past."

Sam said nothing. He simply smiled softly gazing into my eyes with complete understanding. He wrapped his arms around me and pulled me close. I lifted my head, with my eyes still full with warm tears of surrender and he kissed me long, tenderly and passionately. Time stood still as a precious memory was etched forever into our overflowing hearts.

"PAIN AND TRAUMA BURIED ALIVE
NEVER DIE AND WILL ALWAYS
SEEK TO BE RELEASED
SO WE CAN FULLY HEAL.
SOMETIMES THIS RELEASE
IS TRIGGERED BY THE MOST
UNLIKELY PERSON OR OCCURRENCE
AND NEEDS TO BE MEDITATED ON
SO AS NOT TO CONTAMINATE
NEW RELATIONSHIPS
OR MISCONSTRUE NEW EXPERIENCES."

# Rainbow Rider

"Why do you have to overanalyze everything?" demanded my frustrated and hypercritical ego-self. "Maybe there's not always a meaning for everything that happens or in every single creation in the world. Maybe there's just randomness happening and no matter how hard you try, you'll never find the answers you're looking for. Here we are scaling the top of a beautiful mountain and you have to start trying to figure out why God created fall foliage. I mean really; are you kidding me?"

"I am forty-eight years old," my essential-self gently and patiently replied. "This argument of yours, my dear ego, has been going on since I was a kid and my response is always the same. I believe with an absolute knowingness that everything happens for a reason, and all that God created has a purpose. I love trying to figure out the whys of it all. I may not always find the answers but I enjoy the process of exploration. I do find some answers and eventually, maybe not in this lifetime, I am certain that I will find all of them. I completely enjoy the childlike playfulness that you (my ego) bring to this life's experiences. It really helps me appreciate everything this world has to offer. However, seeing the world through spiritual eyes brings more meaning and fulfillment to my time here. So why don't you just settle down and accept this once and for all."

My rebuttal seemed to silence that familiar conflict that goes on from time to time in my thoughts, and I was able to I get back to the moment at hand. It was a picturesque day in early October. Sam and I had taken a leisurely drive up to the mountains to stay a couple of nights at our favorite bed and breakfast. Once we settled into our room, we drove to the local ski resort. They were having an Oktoberfest celebration and offering ski lift rides to the top of the mountain in order to enjoy the magnificent burst of color that exploded throughout the countryside. Hundreds of trees, arms lifted up to the heavens, and roots nestled against the breast of the earth, proudly showcased their brilliant garments.

It was during our slow, steady climb that I began to wonder what purpose this all had. Why *did* God create fall foliage? It happens every year and yet year after year we are mesmerized by this masterpiece that is miraculously orchestrated. The lush greens of summer give way to the reds, oranges, and yellows of autumn, taking our breath away. I felt a wonderful, amazing energy as I breathed in each and every hue. The sun felt warm on my skin and yet the air was crisp, hinting of a long winter chill that would soon grip the Northeast U.S., leaving many of us longing for the first bud break.

We ascended higher and higher until eventually the view allowed me to experience a sensation of flying, no longer bound by the limitations of my physical form. I began lifting up and out of my body, drifting and swirling in and out of the clouds, the trees, the plants, and the animals. I felt myself becoming one with all that surrounded me. As my astral journey continued I felt electrified, renewed, and incredibly alive. It was then that I began to seek the answer to my question.

"So tell me, why?"

A quiet, soft and loving voice that came from a place both outside and inside of my being began to speak.

"Color ... it's all about color. You need color in order for you to be healthy. Think of the energy system."

"Oh, you mean the chakra system," I quipped, envisioning the seven vortexes of energy that run down the midline of the body.

*The chakras are the spiritual body that underlies the physical. The lower three have more to do with physical issues and the upper three with spiritual ones, and the heart center is the bridge between the two. I know from my study of the energy system that each chakra has a color associated with it. The first chakra is red, and located at the base of the spine—the second is orange, then yellow, green, blue, indigo, and the final chakra is white or sometimes purple—located at the crown of the head. Each chakra is affected by different life issues. For example the first chakra, also called the root chakra, can become weakened if you suffered abuse as a child. The fifth chakra, AKA the throat chakra, will not function properly if you fail to speak your truth and hold a lot of things inside. Sometimes we find ourselves drawn to a particular color because the chakra associated with it is in need of balance or healing.*

"Yes, the chakra system," my spirit companion continued. "Human beings are always drawn to color without really understanding why. Think of a beautiful summer sunrise. In the morning, as the sun rises, the first color you see is red, then orange, then yellow—the colors of the first three chakras. Your energy system is awakened. As the world turns from darkness to light, the green of the tree is illumined. You can see deep blue and hints of indigo in the sky, wispy, white clouds, and almost all of the chakra colors in the flowers that adorn gardens and fields everywhere. You feel charged, alive, and energized. Now think of a sunset. Everything happens in reverse. The bright yellow sun descends, giving way to orange, and then red until light becomes darkness and the energy system sleeps.

"Wow that is so cool," I thought. "God sure is a Master Creator. How did He think this stuff up? I have a feeling that question may be one I will never find the answer to."

"Now imagine it is the dead of winter. The sky is grey much of the time. The leaves have long since fallen from the trees. Their skeletal branches are dull and seem lifeless and vulnerable as dark winter storms challenge their will. The colorful artist's pallet that God uses to create seems to be lost. Your energy wanes a bit as the long months of winter carry on; and yet a gentle introspection consumes your spirit as you find time to go within, set new goals, dream new dreams, or renew old ones. It is a time for rest and peace. It is necessary and filled with stillness pregnant with possibilities. As you linger within, in the garden of your soul's light, the outward grey of the landscape propels you to conjure up visions of tulips and daffodils. Eventually, these precious flowers emerging finally spark the beginning of your return to a world of color and the birthing of all you have gestated during your time of respite. It returns just in time.

Fall foliage is God's way of supercharging your energy system in order to take you through those dark and colorless months of winter. In one magnificent explosion of color you are lifted up and infused with an unforgettable memory. A rainbow envelops your being, and you feel awestruck at God's majesty. Power and strength build as your spiritual and physical bodies are renewed and refreshed. All of the colors intermingle with the air as it moves through your breath and into every cell of your body, preparing you for the next part of your journey; a journey that will take you into a kind of mortal slumber and on to an inevitable rebirth. You will move through the doorway of introspection and emerge like a bud of a flower unfolding with the urging of the sun's light. The pendulum shifts. Yin gives way to yang. Dreams manifest and God's world continues to be a perfect, mysterious miracle."

"THERE ARE
ABSOLUTELY NO COINCIDENCES.
I AM ALWAYS AMAZED
AT THE INSIGHTS AND ANSWERS
I RECEIVE
WHEN I TAKE THE TIME TO ASK!"

# *Body Language*

*T*he halls in my children's high school appeared to be mysteriously lengthening as I struggled to find my way out of the building and back to my car. It had been six months since my operation and the pain in my leg and hip were getting worse and worse, rather than better. I instinctively knew something was terribly wrong, but I battled back against the idea that I might have to revisit yet another surgery and long rehabilitation. I managed to finally reach my car. I slumped into the front seat, dropped my head forward against the steering wheel and cried tears of gratitude that the pain had subsided, if only for a moment, and tears of frustration over a healing that seemed elusive at best. I was so tired of being in pain. It wasn't supposed to hurt like this so long after having a total hip replacement. As I fell more and more deeply into my feelings of despair, my mind slipped back to that time six months earlier.

*From the moment I awoke in the recovery room, there was an excruciating pain in my leg. I told the nurse, and she of course, said it was normal. Despite the drugs and aftereffect of the anesthesia, that was the first time I was acutely aware that something had gone wrong. Once I was back in my room, my doctor, Dr. Harriman, came to see me. He reached down and moved my leg slightly, and pain shot like a rocket from my leg deep into every nerve ending in my brain.*

*"Wow, that's a lot of pain!" acknowledged Dr. Harriman. "I am going to order some x-rays just to make sure everything is OK. Beginning tomorrow, however, I'll be out of town for a week, so I won't be around. I'll see you when I get back."*

*So began my ordeal. Each nurse came and went, and I continued to tell them that Dr. Harriman had ordered x-rays and inquired as to why they weren't being done. The same response was delivered over and over; "I don't know. I will check into it."*

*"Hi, Ms. Burrough, my name is Casey, the head nurse on duty today. I checked your chart and there is no record of x-rays having been ordered. Maybe you were mistaken."*

*"No, I am not mistaken," I winced fighting back tears and trying to be strong and assertive, even though I felt inside like a frightened, vulnerable child. "He told me he was ordering x-rays to make sure nothing was wrong. The pain is unbearable, and I'm getting really scared. I know something is not right."*

*"You've just had a major surgery. Pain like this is to be expected," she scolded as if I were some insubordinate child. "I'll get the doctor who is presently on the floor, and he can prescribe more pain medication."*

*"Ms. Burrough, I am Dr. Devler. I understand you are having a lot of pain. Let's take a look."*

*He checked my incision. There was a long nasty looking wound on the side of my left thigh where the surgical team had reached inside of my body, popped out the joint, sawed off the head of my femur bone, drilled a long hole into the shaft of the femur, and inserted my shiny, brand new hip.*

*"Everything looks fine. We'll do a blood test to check for infection, and I am going to prescribe Oxycontin for the pain and also muscle relaxers. That's in addition to the morphine and Percocet that you are already taking."*

*"But wait," I called as he turned to leave without even bothering to allow me a chance to voice my concerns. "Dr. Harriman said he wanted x-rays done and they were never done. I am really sure something is wrong."*

*"You need to relax. The post operative x-rays must have looked fine.*

There is no need for more," he impatiently retorted and quickly left the room.

"Why won't anyone listen to me?" I screamed frantically inside my troubled mind, as fear gathered in every part of my broken body. "I think I am dying and no one cares. What if I die? What will happen to my kids? I can't die. I have to get someone to hear me. I have to find a way to fix this."

Obviously, my thoughts were becoming irrational at times, due to the incessant terror that was gripping me, but my resolve and absolute belief that something was terribly wrong was far from irrational. I was eventually transferred to the rehabilitation part of the hospital and my nightmare continued. My mobility status was 40% weight-bearing. Being the athlete and competitor I have always been, I was determined to do the best job I could in rehab. I made sure that I took my pain medication right before each session so I could get through it successfully. While working with the physical therapists and occupational therapists, I stuffed my pain deep inside and courageously completed every exercise they gave me, working tirelessly and torturously through the endless tears. One time I brought their attention to the fact that an eighty-year-old woman next to me had no trouble doing leg raises and I, being only forty-eight, felt like I was climbing Mount Everest. Yet, again my concerns fell on deaf ears. The days passed slowly and painfully and finally, I was released from the hospital.

Once at home, with no wheelchair to help me to get around, I had to start trying to function in my life. I couldn't! After being home one day, I called my doctor. By the time he got on the phone I could barely speak but I managed to convey to him with a cracking, trembling voice that I had to see him that day!

A friend of mine drove me to the appointment. Hobbling into the *office on crutches, I barely got to the bathroom in time before I started to vomit violently from all of the ineffective pain medication I was taking.*

*"OK," Dr Harriman stated. "I'm going to do a blood test to check for infection and change your pain medication."*

*"No!" I replied, angrily. "You are going to do an x-ray. Something is wrong and has been wrong since the day of the operation."*

*He reluctantly agreed and I was ushered down the hall. The technician took one x-ray, checked it and came back and took another and then another all the while with an evident look of concern on his face. "They found something. I knew it."*

*"You must have broken your leg when you fell," Dr. Harriman surmised, as he looked at the x-rays.*

*"What are you talking about? I never fell," I shot back with hostility. "This pain has been the same pain all along. It has just gotten worse."*

*I guess he was trying to cover his butt but at that point I didn't care; I just wanted him to fix the problem. After consulting with other specialists he decided to go back into the same incision site and do an internal fixation (putting a wire around the femur to hold the fracture together). He did the procedure immediately and for a short time I had a reprieve from the intense pain. He assured me that the prosthesis was still in place and everything would be OK from then on.*

*Hardly! Over the next six months, the limp never went away. I walked as if I was stepping off a curb and my left foot seemed to turn inward as I walked. I refused to go back to Dr. Harriman because my trust in him had been totally shattered. I tried to explain to the new orthopedist that I thought the prosthesis had slipped into the shaft of the femur and medially rotated. He took several x-rays over the course of a few months and insisted each time that I was wrong. I knew I wasn't!*

I lifted my head from the steering wheel, reached for my cell phone and made an urgent call to my doctor, the current orthopedist, Dr. Benson. I insisted on seeing him right away. The receptionist told me to come right in. After reiterating my same complaints and suspicions, Dr. Benson decided that I needed to see a revision specialist because he could not help me. (A revision specialist is someone who revises a previous surgery.) I knew that being referred to a revision specialist meant that there was a good chance I was headed for another major surgery. Surprisingly, I was not as horrified as I thought I would be. All I wanted, at this point, was to be able to live my life without the constant, dark cloud of pain and disability.

"Ms. Burrough, my name is Dr. Meeren. I have looked at your x-rays," he said, as he pushed them up into the light so he could show me what he had found. "The whole thing is pretty much a mess. The prosthesis slipped into the shaft of the femur and it twisted medially. Your leg is significantly shorter and walking normally is impossible the way things are now. We need to pull the whole thing out and do it over." Amazingly, my body had told me exactly what was wrong! Dr. Meeren just confirmed it.

Dr. Meeren was a specialist who worked in a prominent hospital in Manhattan and he also taught at a local university. He came highly recommended and my intuition this time was to trust him. Almost one year after the first surgery, I had the second one. I woke up in the recovery room completely certain that it was a success and I was on the road to recovery. The day after the operation Dr. Meeren came to see me. He exuded an air of confidence. He was handsome with thick, curly auburn hair and spoke with a strong European accent.

"Dr. Meeren," I gushed. "Everything is so perfect!"

"No, Drusilla everything is not perfect," he responded in his adorable melodic tone, "It is PRECISE! Orthopedics is always about function. If there is even a slight bit of imprecision you cannot function properly."

"Well OK," I said, "It is perfectly precise then!" He smiled, shook my hand and said, "I'll see you in five weeks."

> "MY INTUITION CONSISTENTLY
> LEADS ME ON THE PATH OF TRUTH,
> WISDOM AND ENLIGHTENMENT.
> MY BODY ALSO CONTINUOUSLY
> SPEAKS TO ME AND TELLS ME WHAT
> IT NEEDS TO GET AND STAY HEALTHY.
> I TRUST THAT VOICE."

# *Speak Now or Forever Hold Regret*

*I*n one explosive moment, I burst into a firestorm of angry, wounded tears. Thrusting my chair backwards I leapt up, charged for the patio doors that led back into the house and made a dramatic exit. Sam was left in a cloud of confusion and bewilderment. Mom and Dad, on the other hand, were not unfamiliar with the fallout that often occurred when Dad got his back up on certain issues, grabbed his powerful, paternal sword, and unintentionally set forth to reduce any one of us to the intimidated, wounded child of yesteryear.

Sam had just met my parents for the first time at their home in Melbourne, Florida in 2001. Everything was going smoothly. It was obvious that they adored him right from the start. Sam and I had spent a leisurely day at Cocoa Beach, and were lucky enough to see a space shuttle launch at Cape Canaveral. Sam was in heaven as it just happened to be on his "bucket list," and coincidently occurred during our trip to Florida. We headed back to my parents' house in the late afternoon, and were geared up and ready for cocktail hour.

Mom is a master at creating a spread of delicacies fit for a king or queen. We all grabbed our drinks of choice and settled into a nice comfy chair on the porch. That small space right off the living room is such a peaceful, serene spot. The floor-to-ceiling glass windows showcase a little man-made pond that is always a playground for the most unusual looking ducks I have ever seen, as well as graceful egrets, and an occasional pelican. We were having a wonderful time enjoying the tasty appetizers Mom had prepared, and talking about anything and everything. Eventually the conversation took a spiritual turn. This was never a good idea.

As I have previously mentioned, though I was raised Catholic, I had moved beyond the confines of organized religion. I had studied many different religions and no longer defined myself as only Catholic, but as a deeply spiritual woman who saw truth and divinity in many religions or in no religion at all. Dad didn't understand. He and Mom were very involved in the church. Mom was more liberal and she was open to other things, and was curious and eager to learn about Eastern religions and other spiritual philosophies. Dad was not. I believe he had a lot of fear as many Catholics do, and anything other than the doctrine taught by the Catholic church was certain to be "Satan's work."

All seven of my siblings and I were always trying to gain my dad's approval and praise. It was not easily achieved, if ever at all. He wasn't able to accept that his children might, perhaps, be able to teach him something or that our paths, though different from his, might be equally as worthwhile and purposeful. That didn't stop us from trying and it almost always led to hurt feelings, anger, misunderstanding or a meltdown like the one that had just occurred, when Dad criticized my spiritual perspective.

"Are you OK," Sam asked as he wrapped his arms around me, lifting me from the bed and trying to calm the avalanche of toxic, turbulent tears that were causing a trembling and tightening in every part of my body. "You seemed to be holding your own in that conversation. You know what you believe in! What you said was strong and you presented your point of view with conviction. So what happened?"

"You don't know my dad. You don't know what he does to all of us. I know he doesn't mean to cause us pain but he does. His words are so sharp and they cut so deep. I don't understand why he doesn't even try to see my point of view. He doesn't take the time to know me. He has never known who I am and it hurts. I want him to really see me, Dru, and to see that

I am different and beautiful and that what I believe in is just as valuable as what he believes in. I am insulted and hurt that he could believe for a second that what I do or who I am is 'Satan's work.' He has no faith in me. He never has, so I don't even know why I try. It's hopeless."

Just talking about it helped to still the treacherous waters of abandonment and rejection in which I was drowning. "I'm OK," I sniffed. "I have to be. We should get back out there. I just need to pretend it didn't happen and everything will be OK."

"You need to talk to your dad," Steve urged. "You can't just ignore this. Who knows how much time we have with our parents or with anybody for that matter? You really need to say something before we leave."

"No way, never, I can't! That's not how it works. Whenever he does something like this we get upset and then we forget about it and move on. No one ever talks to him about it. It's too scary."

Sam didn't push the issue but he most certainly planted a seed of possibility in my mind and awakened in me a voice from somewhere inside my wounded heart that whispered "He's right! It will be OK. Talk to dad before it's too late."

The following day we were getting ready to head back to NY. Nothing was said about the incident the day before and we all acted as if it hadn't happened. However, my insistent new companion who had taken up residence in my thoughts continued to encourage me to talk to my dad and tell him how I feel. Sam, Mom, Dad and I were all about to leave the porch, and go out to our car so we could say our good-byes. Mom and Sam left first. I was right behind them and Dad was behind me. My heart was pounding as a frenzied swarm of butterflies swirled wildly in my stomach. I turned abruptly and faced my dad looking directly into his eyes. I had no idea what I was going to say but I had to say something.

"Dad, I'm sorry about yesterday."

"No, I'm sorry," he interrupted. "Sometimes I just put my big, fat foot in my mouth and I don't know what I'm saying. I want you to know something, Dru. I am so proud of you. I am proud of the way you have raised your children, and I am proud of who you are. I love you."

I was stunned! "Did he really just say what I think he said?" I was overwhelmed with emotion, somewhat dazed and absolutely joyful. "He really does love me. He really had taken the time to know who I am." It was just his "stuff," his own baggage that always got in the way of telling me. I threw my arms around his neck and tearfully echoed those powerful, healing words, "I love you too, Dad!"

Dad passed away a few years later and I am so grateful I that I listened to Sam and to my own heart, and summoned forth the courage to take the action that led to one of the most amazing moments of my life. If I had not done so, I think I would have always felt that there was much unfinished business between me and my dad. That moment gave me closure that would most certainly have been absent and mourned during that sad and difficult time when my daddy passed from this world, and even more so in the months and years that followed.

> "ASSUMING THAT SOMEONE IN MY
> LIFE KNOWS HOW I FEEL, OR THAT I
> KNOW HOW THEY FEEL, MAY LEAVE US
> BOTH WITHOUT THE TRUTH.
> DON'T WAIT UNTIL IT'S TOO LATE.
> SPEAK UP ... TODAY!"

*I wrote the following piece about my dad when I was in my mid-twenties. The next two poems after that are about the night he passed away and also my thoughts, prayers and concerns about whether he was OK after his crossing over to spirit. For some reason, most of the time that I sit down to write about him my thoughts and words come in the form of poetry. I'm not sure why but I guess that's just inspiration, being "in spirit" with my dad for just a moment.*

# He is to Me

He is a man who loves with great intensity;
His heart is so full of love, kindness and compassion.
In fact, I feel sometimes that his heart must be ready to burst
Because so much of his love remains inside—
Inside a prison of his own making,
Unable to really reach out and touch
The ones so very dear to him.

Yet, with each passing year the bars of the prison
Grow weaker …
The bars that incarcerate the true substance of his being
Give way …
To the strength and fervor of the love that exists within.

How different it all seems from the innocent years of childhood
When adult and child seemed completely unrelated.
Yet, with the help of God, I now see the child within the man,
And suddenly, I seem to understand and cherish
All of the vivid memories of those confusing times
When everything seemed so unclear.
For Dad, it was not easy to express love the way we needed him to.

He did his best!
Life is short and mere words have yet to capture
The height of my gratitude and love for him.
Yet, somehow …
He knows …
My dad knows.

"WHEN A PARENT'S LOVE
IS HARD TO SEE
AND FEEL ON THE SURFACE,
WE NEED TO LOOK MORE DEEPLY
AT THEM AND THEIR PAST
WITH COMPASSION
AND UNDERSTANDING
AND WE WILL MOST LIKELY FIND
WHAT WE ARE LOOKING FOR—
THEIR LOVE."

# *Full Moon*
### (My dad moves into the light)

The lights went out as they did each night;
My children had just gone to bed.
I sat in the darkness gazing at the moon
Thinking about what Mom had said.

All eight of her children continuously asked,
"How's Dad; do you need us to come?"
Over and over in her soft, sweet tone
She said "He's fine and enjoying the sun."

The day was Father's Day; I called my dad,
And my mom said, "I think it's time—
Dialysis isn't working—he's slipping away.
Whenever you can get here is fine.

The moon was full on that warm June night;
I sat in the moonlight and cried.
The silence was broken by the sound of the phone.
And my brother said that Dad had just died.

I hung up the phone and collapsed on the couch.
My heart ached, I didn't say goodbye.
Staring solemnly at the moon, I knew he was there;
My dad came to be by my side.

Through my grief I understood that the moon was his gift—
A sign that he'd always be here.
So over the years, when the moon is full,
I feel his presence and I know he is near.

Later I learned that he loved the full moon,
And each month when it was beautiful and bright,
He'd sing to my mom and profess his love,
As he did for me that sad June night.

"WHEN SOMEONE I LOVE
TRANSITIONS TO THAT
INVISIBLE PLACE,
IF I PAY CLOSE ATTENTION,
LISTEN CAREFULLY
AND WATCH FOR SIGNS,
I KNOW THAT THEY WILL ALWAYS
LET ME KNOW
THEY ARE CLOSE
AND ARE WELL, AND HAPPY."

# *Only Love*

Dear God, I ask, is he OK?
Did you give him back his smile?
Can he fly throughout the heavens now,
Or must he rest for a little while?

Is he at peace and free from pain?
Lord, I really need to know.
Did you give him a grand celebration
In the light of your angels' glow?

"Be assured, my child." I hear God say
That nothing much has changed.
He remains who he's always been—
Just a few things were rearranged.

He hears your prayers and feels your love,
And he smiles with joy and peace.
His birth was grand and glorious
As his spirit was finally released.

And yes, he flies through the heavens now
Like a carefree happy child.
Yet, he journeys back to the ones he loves
To visit for a little while.

Suddenly I feel him close to me.
I hear his voice as he begins to say,
"If only you could see the beauty here
All your tears would fade away.

I can tell you for sure, there is no death,
Only birth to a different place.
And the only thing that is real is love,
Not even time or space.

So please don't grieve, and please don't cry
For this is where I must be.
Find me in the wind, the clouds and the air—
In the rivers, streams and the sea.

Please celebrate my life, not death.
Be happy and filled with love.
Hope and dream, and live your life.
I'll be watching from the heavens above."

"I HAVE COME TO UNDERSTAND
THAT THE ONLY THING
THAT IS TRULY REAL IS LOVE,
AND ONLY LOVE.
EVERYTHING ELSE IS AN ILLUSION
INCLUDING FEAR,
HATE, ANGER, JEALOUSY, ETC.
THESE ARE QUALITIES BORN OF
THE EGO, NOT THE SOUL.
THE SOUL WAS CREATED BY,
AND THEREFORE IS
AND WILL ALWAYS BE,
"ONLY LOVE."

# The God Box

$S$ome dreams are born in the fantasy of a child's mind wishing and hoping for: fairy tales to come true, princes and princesses, slaying dragons, changing the world, becoming president, or simply being a mom or dad. Some dreams are born through gathering of wisdom, knowledge of wrongs that should be righted, a world that needs healing, or the entrance of child into your life sparking a dream for the hopes and happiness of a young boy or girl. And then, some dreams are born out of an ironic twist of fate never anticipated, never fathomed, and never in a million years thought possible—a dream that prays for a return to what was, an understanding of what is, and courage to let it all go in faith knowing in the end it will all make sense. I have dreamed such dreams in my life, but the latter has been a dream draped in misery, pain, and anguish—a dream that offers little possibility that I have the key to unlock it.

My son, Jake Asher, was born April 6, 1986 after two-and-a-half years of all-consuming, infertility treatments. What an amazing Sunday that was! He came into this world a little after 12:00 noon. He was a beautiful, tiny angel only about six pounds, two ounces. He was perfect in every way. He inspired awe as people stopped me on the street and continuously described him as "angelic." They would ask if he was always so good. "Does he ever cry?" He didn't. He was my manifestation of complete and utter peace in a world, and a marriage that was not at all peaceful.

"Here's a picture of creation!" he announced one afternoon when he was only four. It was hard to understand from a four-year-old's drawing, so he described it. "Here's Jesus holding the formula for creation … and over here is a bad man who is trying to knock the formula out of Jesus's hand but up here," he continued, "is the world. He already finished it and we are all living there and we're safe."

Jake was a gentle, sweet, calm, soul, and not much could upset or anger him. He played soccer as a child and would run down the field with his head swaying from side to side as he felt the cool breeze on his face. It was more like he was jogging in the park rather than playing in a soccer game. Nevertheless, he played a mean game of soccer. There was another boy on his team who was a bit nasty, and taunted Jake all the time. Jake just usually ignored him. However, one day in late fall when he was about eight years old, I looked out the window and saw him on top of this kid letting him have it. I went flying out the door, but by the time I got to him he was sobbing and trembling. I held him in my arms as he cried. He kept saying he was sorry and later wrote a letter to me telling me what he learned. He said, "Hurting somebody doesn't feel good and it's OK to be angry. But, I don't think I should let it out like that."

In sixth grade his teacher announced that it was "Act of Kindness Day." Jake spent the day searching for a way to be kind to someone. On the way home on the bus some boys were picking on another small boy. Jake stood up for him and told them to leave him alone. My son was a big kid, and even though he was peaceful, not many would mess with him.

Just a few years ago, in May, 2003, when I was in the hospital after having hip surgery, I lay in bed with tubes and machines everywhere. Jake walked in, tears welled in his eyes, and worry shrouded his handsome face. He sat down, took my hand, handed me a small stuffed dog, and through his tears he said, "Mom, I love you so much!"

His senior year in high school 2003-2004 was not exactly an easy time. He was struggling with the fear of college and of becoming a man like most young boys his age. We battled that year a bit, but nothing earth-shattering or unusual. I thought he should get a job since he got out of school at 12:00 noon, clean his room, wash the dishes after he used them—all pretty typical teenage stuff to fight over. Then in June, 2004 my daughter Brianne, who is a year younger, got a job as a camp counselor. She evaluated what her contract would yield monetarily, and then came to me with a plan.

"I need this much for school clothes, this much for Christmas, and this much for a cell phone annual contract. Can I get a cell phone?" she asked.

"Absolutely," I said, so proud of her mature and organized plan.

When Jake heard this, he informed me that if Brianne could get a cell phone, he should be able to have one as well. I told him no. He had no job, no way to pay for it, and I couldn't afford it. He pleaded and litigated his case, and in the end I still said, "No!" I had no choice. Then, one afternoon in August, 2004 he said, "If you don't get me a cell phone, you will never see me again."

"Pretty dramatic," I thought, but dismissed it as yet one more attempt to get his way. The next day when I was at work he packed his things and left. He moved in with his dad.

At the time of this writing, I am now approaching the fifth Christmas without my son in my life. I have not seen him at all in those five years and have spoken to him only three times for no more than five minutes at a time. I call him at least once a month. He doesn't answer his phone, so I leave messages of love—a continuous affirmation that my love will always remain the same no matter what—and that I am here if, and when he is ready to talk. I don't know why he is so angry or so adamant that he does not need me in his life. It has to be more than a silly cell phone. He refuses to explain even to my daughters when they ask, and so, I am left with only prayers and unanswered questions. I have cried deep, boring, and anguished tears for hours and hours on end. My tears, though cleansing and purging, have yielded little peace. My dream to return to what was, or even to rebuild what is, remains in the ethers of the un-manifest world. So it is that this dream takes up residence in my "God Box," a small wooden box that I keep on my dresser. In it are all things or issues in my life that I cannot fix. I write a brief letter to God about the issue, seal the letter, and turn it over to Him. One sorrowful and mournful day a few years ago I wrote a letter to God about the painful situation with Jake. I included a picture of my son with his arms around me. It was so hard to let go. I had been so sure I could make it OK. I couldn't. I placed a tender kiss on the envelope, placed it in the Box, slowly closed it, and then sadly released it. My dream now rests peacefully in that Box and though tears still rise and fall with thoughts of my precious baby boy, I know I must live my life with joy, purpose, and a sense of inner peace, trying always to stay in gratitude for what is, and prayerful for what I hope will be.

> "IN PAINFUL CIRCUMSTANCES SUCH AS THIS, WHERE THERE ARE NO CLEAR ANSWERS, I HAVE LEARNED TO TURN THE SITUATION OVER TO GOD AND TRUST THAT THERE IS A LARGER PICTURE I CANNOT YET SEE. I WILL CHOOSE LOVE, FORGIVENESS AND FAITH, AND BELIEVE THAT ONE DAY, I WILL UNDERSTAND."

# *Touching Words (God Box Two)*

*T*he bright, luminescent autumn sun hung lazily in the western sky as I sat leisurely in our backyard. A chilly breeze wisped through the colorful canopy as it tried ineffectively to hold on to its slowly withering, thinning garment. Yellow, red, and orange leaves floated and danced aimlessly on wind currents, softly finding their way to the expectant, cool earth. Feeling nostalgic for so many seasons that had come and gone in my life brought memories of younger days. I thought about my childhood when my brothers, sisters, and I would rake and pile up mounds of crunchy leaves, run briskly with wild abandon, and jump joyfully into the middle. The earthy smell, the crackling sound and later the sight of thick white smoky swirls, and the cannabis-like aroma as my dad burned away the piles, etched a lasting memory in my mind. That reminiscence today brings up feelings of innocence, ease, and simplicity that seem at times, absent as I deal with the growing aches and pains associated with the autumn of my own life. My thoughts then moved forward in time when my own children were young, and they continued this timeless tradition minus the burning of the leaves, of course. I felt a gentle smile curl the corners of my mouth as I relished every tiny detail of their happy smiles and their jubilant laughter. I mentally studied each of my children, remembering clearly that younger version of the adults they now are today.

Brianne has graduated from college, Magna Cum Laude, and is a young professional living in Manhattan. She has landed her dream job and is working as a financial analyst for an international company. Allison is in her senior year in college and is studying neuroscience. She has lofty dreams of teaching the world what she has always believed. She has intuitively known that we can create the life we want by the power of our thoughts, and she believes that medication is much overprescribed in our country. Her study is proving these things to be true. Then, there is Jake. My pleasant, contented smile disappears as I am forced into the harsh reality that it has been almost seven long, sad years since I have seen my son. I am still unaware of why he chose to leave my life. He has still not told anyone, not even his sisters, and he continues to refuse to talk about it.

"Oh Jake, what happened to you? What happened to us," I plead, lifting my eyes to the heavens, hoping that somehow, my voice will penetrate the empty space between us and reach his beautiful heart and confused mind.

Over the years he has been gone, I have not stopped trying to reach out to him. I continue to call regularly leaving messages on his cell phone. I tell him how much I miss him and that I will never stop loving him, no matter what. I tell him I am here for him if he ever needs me and when and if he is ready to come back, my heart is always open to him. Sometimes he answers the phone but when he hears my voice he hangs up. I send gifts to him for his birthday and Christmas, and even make him an Easter basket every year. One Christmas I spent hours and days putting together a picture album of him and us so he might remember how much I love him and what an incredible family he has. The girls deliver my gifts. They tell me he liked them, but I never receive a call or a thank you. When he received the album, he looked carefully through the pages and then said to his sisters, "I don't remember any of this." I wonder if my little boy is, somehow, being held prisoner in his adult body, and I pray that he will escape and remember who he is and how much he is loved.

My God box continues to hold my pain, and feelings of loss and helplessness about my son. I keep him tucked away inside my heart in a special place where I can nurture him and love him without being able to see or touch him. I believe that on some level, his soul knows how much I care. I have faith that someday he will come back to me. I try not to dwell on the devastation I feel. If I did, I could not live my life and be the joyful person I choose to be. I have much to be grateful for, and I focus on those things leaving this painful situation to God.

Lowering my head to my chest brought me back to the present moment, and I was gratefully released from my disturbing thoughts. I glanced down at my cell phone lying on the table in front of me. Without thinking I picked it up and dialed Jake's number. He did not answer, and it went to his voicemail. I decided not to leave a message because I thought I would be too upset and not able to talk. A few minutes later my phone rang. In disbelief I saw that it was a call coming in from my son.

"Hello?" I nervously answered.

"Did someone call from this number?" he inquired, obviously not knowing it was me. I felt a letdown and despair as I realized that when he learned it was me, he would hang up, as usual.

"Jake, its Mom," I responded, preparing myself for those dreaded words flashing on my cell—"call ended." They never came.

I jumped from my chair, my heart racing wildly as a surging, bloody fire flowed to my neck and face. I began wandering around the backyard trying to stay as calm as I possibly could.

"What now? What would I say? How can I touch my son and hold him in my arms when all I have are my words and the sound of my voice? How can I make him understand how much I adore him?"

"How are you, Jake?" was all I could come up with. "Geez, how pathetic," I thought.

"I'm fine, Mom," he answered sending adrenalin coursing through my body as I tried desperately to find the right words.

"Jake, I miss you so much. I don't understand why you left. I'm sure there are things I did or didn't do that made you leave, and whatever they are, I am sorry," I offered to him, my voice cracking and trembling as I fought to hold back the tears that would not be restrained.

"It's not you, Mom. It's me. You didn't do anything. I'm sorry I put you through all this."

"I just want you in my life, honey," I responded. "I want to love you and support you. The other day I did a meditation and you came to me. You were my little baby boy again, and I held you in my arms. I looked into your eyes and I could see the love in yours. It was so real. I just want a chance to start over. I want us to be able to share this life together," I wept, clutching at my aching heart.

"I don't know why you don't just move on from me, Mom. I'm not the person you think I am."

"You are my son! You are my precious little boy! I will never ever, ever, ever move on from you! Nothing you could do or say would ever make me stop loving you. I know who you are. I remember who you are. I remember your beautiful, loving heart. I remember when you were in sixth grade and Ms. Evans, your teacher, told the class it was 'Act of Kindness Day' and you were all to find a way to be kind. On the way home, there was a kid on the bus being picked on, you stood up for him, and put the bullies in their place. I remember when Bri's friend Penny was being teased by girls on the playground and you came over and told them to leave Penny alone. I remember when I had hip replacement, right before you left. You came to the hospital and gave me a stuffed animal that I still have on my bed today. You sat down next to me and started to cry. You put your arms around me and told me how much you loved me. That is you. That is my amazing son who I have held onto over the last six years. I have cherished the memory of those three words you spoke to me that day that came from your precious, loving heart."

I paused for a moment and thought I could hear him sniffling. I waited hoping he would say something. Nothing came and suddenly, there was silence.

"Jake, are you there?"

He was gone. I tried calling back but he did not answer. I came back to the patio and sat down next to Sam. Tears were now flowing from that space inside of me where my little boy has resided for the past several years. I crossed my arms over my abdomen and pressed hard and tight in a fruitless attempt to dull the pain and ease the anguish that was twisting relentlessly in my gut. My feelings and emotions were complicated, and confusing. I was so grateful for having had a chance to talk to him. I was comforted in knowing that, for at least a moment, he didn't blame me for what had become of his life. I was sad at hearing what sounded like depression and hopelessness in his voice. Yet, my profound feeling of hope likened itself to those first crimson rays of glorious morning light that promise the birth of a new day, a new life, and a chance to begin anew.

A week has passed, and though I have attempted to call him again, I cannot reach him. I remain, once again, in this surreal space of life without my firstborn child. Yet, my faith and my hope remain strong. I believe in him. I believe in us and what we had, and I continue to pray,

"God, please help Jake to find his way back home. Amen."

"I WILL NEVER GIVE UP ON
THOSE I LOVE—NO MATTER WHAT.
MIRACLES HAPPEN
WHEN YOU LEAST EXPECT THEM.
I AWAIT, STILL,
MY FINAL MIRACLE
BELIEVING FULLY THAT
THE SITUATION IS IN GOD'S HANDS,
AND HE WILL TAKE CARE OF IT
IN HIS OWN TIME."

# *Tomorrow is Today (God Box Three)*

$\mathcal{T}$he day started like most others until the phone rang.

"Hi Dru, it's Marianna," my sister said. "I have some sad news. Jake's cousin, Jim, passed away suddenly. No one knows what happened yet, but he is gone."

"Oh my God, are you serious?" I responded. "How can that be? He was so young," I said completely shocked and devastated.

I didn't see Jim much after the divorce. Yet, every time I did, he would tell me that I would always be his cousin no matter what, even if I was still not technically part of the family. He had been married a couple of times over the years, and I believe he had a total of four beautiful children—three girls and a boy. His youngest was only four years old when Jim left this world at forty-eight years old.

The weekend of the wake and funeral left me trying to comprehend how this could have happened to that cute bushy-haired ten-year-old little boy I met so many years ago. Even after my sister Marianna, who happens to be married to my ex's first cousin Tim, called to break the devastating news to me, I still couldn't believe it. Apparently Jim had some kind of seizure, hit his head on the pavement, and died several hours later. I couldn't help but think of his kids. How would they cope? I couldn't imagine how his entire family would handle it either. I wished I could go to the wake and funeral to say goodbye. I was pretty sure the rest of the family would have loved my support but I decided I couldn't. I was again concerned that my presence, after so many years, would create discomfort and might disrupt the solemn and sad occasion.

Both my daughters rushed home—Allison from school in Albany—

Brianne from her home in Manhattan—to be with their dad, brother, grandmother, and the rest of the family. I spent the time—those three long days—asking questions, pondering the mysteries and painful realities of this life in the silence and solitude of my unshared grief.

"Why was his life cut so short?" I questioned. "Am I happy and content with what I have done so far in *my* life? We never know how much time we have here on earth, so I had better not keep putting things off until tomorrow. Tomorrow may never come. I wonder if Jim is regretting not telling certain people how much he loved them. I wonder if he was waiting for just the right time to fulfill his big dream, whatever that might have been."

These kinds of thoughts continued all day Saturday and Sunday, as I considered his family and friends going to the funeral home—saying their final goodbyes to a man, son, brother, father, and friend who left this world far too soon, leaving everyone wishing they had just one more day to tell him how much they loved him. Monday morning arrived, the day of the funeral. Allison had to go back to school on Sunday but Bri took off from work to attend the service. She decided not to go to the luncheon afterward and asked me if I would pick her up at her grandmother's house. My son, Jake was going to take her back to our house but his car broke down.

"Mom, it's Bri. The funeral mass is over and I'm back at grandma's. Can you leave now and come get me?"

"Sure," I responded. "I'm on my way. I should be there in about forty-five minutes."

I hung up the phone and dashed out to the car. I was about three quarters of the way there when I suddenly heard an urgent, commanding inner voice disrupt the sound of my favorite music CD.

"Go see Jake Asher! Go see your son! Don't wait! Go in and see him! As you have learned, tomorrow may never come. It's just Jake and Bri in the house alone. This is the perfect time. Do it! You may not have another chance."

"What if he rejects me again? I don't know if I could handle that. I'm scared," I thought, trembling.

"He's your son. You gave birth to him. Believe that he loves you. Don't think about it, just do it!"

I pulled into the driveway, put the car in park, marched up the front steps, and rang the bell. Bri answered the door.

"What are you doing Mom," she asked in a terrifying tone because anything closer than the curb was off limits to me.

"I'm going to see Jake. I have to do this Bri. He's my son. I love him. I'm prepared for whatever happens but I have to see him. It's been over six years of not even knowing why he left. I don't even think he knows anymore. He needs me. I know he does, and I believe he loves me too."

With Bri noticeably fearful that I would be hurt once again and silently protesting, I walked down the stairs and made a right turn heading toward the back of the basement. Jake was coming toward me and stopped. He looked at me with sad-looking eyes and very little expression. Without hesitating, I walked over to him, reached up and put my arms around his neck and pulled him close.

"I love you Jake," I whispered softly into his ear. "I had to see you. I had to hold you in my arms so that you could feel my love and remember. I will always love you and I will never ever give up on us—never."

"I'm sorry, Mom. I just don't think I can be anything to you. I just don't think I have it in me."

I pulled back from him and looked up into his beautiful blue eyes.

I took his face into my hands and stroked the sides of his lightly bearded countenance. He looked so much more mature since the last time I saw him when he was only eighteen years old. He looked lost and his eyes seemed no longer to have that spark I remember so well from when he was a child. I reached back up and held him again a little tighter. I could feel his arms across my back, ever so lightly but they were there.

"I know you Jake. I know us. I remember your love, and I know with all my heart that you still love me. I will always be there for you—always. I believe that someday you will come back—when you do I will be waiting with my arms wide open—my heart still filled with as much, if not more, love for you than when you left."

Jake continued to say over and over that he was sorry. I don't know what he was sorry for or why. It was not my intention to get into a long conversation or put him on the spot, only to let him feel the touch of a mother's love because I wasn't sure he even remembered what that felt like. He didn't push me away but allowed me to hold him for as long as I wanted. I pulled my arms back, resting my hands on his shoulders, drew back a few inches and reached down and took hold of one of his hands. I brought it up to my lips, kissed it softly, and held it to my cheek as mixed tears of sadness and joy fell gently onto our intertwined fingers. I reached up one more time, embraced my little boy, then looked deeply into his eyes, and affirmed one last time how much I loved him.

"Goodbye for now, Jake," I uttered softly as I turned and silently went back up the stairs and out to my car.

I'm not at all sure what that short time with Jake meant. Did it mean that he was one step closer to retuning to my life? I don't know. Yet, I am profoundly grateful for my inner guidance, the courage I found to heed that still, small, persistent voice, and mostly for the beautiful moment of intimacy I shared with my son. It left me filled with hope. It is my prayer that he too was left with joyful hope as well, an expectation that love can heal broken hearts, and that a mother's unconditional love never dies no matter how much time goes by or how much distance separates mother from child. "God, please take care of my son, keep him safe and help him to remember how amazing he is."

"THE ONLY TIME THAT IS REAL
IS 'NOW,' RIGHT THIS MOMENT.
YESTERDAY AND TOMORROW
ONCE WERE AND WILL BE
**THE EVER-PRESENT 'NOW.'**
I VOW TO NEVER FEEL THE STING
OF REGRET FOR NOT HAVING ACTED,
AND I PROMISE I WILL NOT WAIT FOR
A MOMENT THAT MAY NEVER COME.
I WILL ACT NOW!
I WILL NEVER LOSE HOPE
THAT LOVE CAN MIRACULOUSLY
CREATE A PATH
TO HEALING AND FORGIVENESS.
I LOVE YOU JAKE."

*"In 1997, at age forty-three, I found myself alone, a single mother struggling to understand all that had happened over the past several years, and trying to handle what my life had become. This poem reflects my thoughts many years later."*

# Light at the Core

How did I ever come to that place
Of loneliness, sadness, and tears.
Dreams died slowly, and pain took root
As I drowned in a sea of dark fears.

Single in a personal story of one,
How had I lost my way?
The struggles were endless, the worries too much,
And I begged God, "Please take them away."

Yet, I was the parent of three young lives.
They depended on my strength and my love.
They didn't understand that I was too weak to give.
My only hope was the light from above.

I looked in their eyes filled with wonder and joy,
And the struggle seemed easier to bear.
I taught about how, to find good in the hurt;
I taught them, they have hearts they must share.

Their love became food that renewed my soul;
Their laughter was a fresh flowing stream.
I ate and I drank, and in time, I returned.
Things weren't as bad as they seemed.

I learned over time, that adversity brings growth—
Authenticity replaces untruth.
The months turned to years and my children are grown.
I now cherish those struggles of my youth.

"MOST ALL OF US
HAVE A DARK NIGHT OF THE SOUL
AT ONE TIME OR ANOTHER.
FOCUSING ON THE BEAUTY, LOVE,
AND GOOD IN OUR LIVES
GIVES US HOPE,
CARRIES US THROUGH,
REMINDS US THAT WE
ARE STRONG AND POWERFUL,
AND THAT WE WILL SURVIVE."

# *Indigo Child*

*(Written in first person narrative for, about, and with permission of my daughter, Allison)*

*I* am an "Indigo" child—not a "Crystal" child, although we both have similarities. I learned about this from reading the work of a wonderful author and spiritual teacher named Doreen Virtue. She taught me that Indigos have large penetrating eyes. I do. "If you look deeply," she offers, "you will see a child or young adult far wiser than his or her chronological age. They have the ability to, sort of, hypnotize you, and this allows you to realize in that moment, that your soul has been revealed before a wise, spiritual being. You may not be able to put into words your experience with an Indigo child but you sense something special and magnetic. We are both highly sensitive and psychic."

We, the Indigos, are also warriors and have a fiery temperament. It is really hard for us to tolerate injustice or deception of any kind. We rise up quickly against any individual or institution that lacks integrity. We began incarnating over one hundred years ago with the last of us being born around 2000. To accomplish our goals we needed a strong temper and intense determination, both of which we have. This sometimes caused problems for us in our relationships. I know it did in mine.

Crystal children came after the Indigos and began incarnating from about 2000. They are more blissful and even-tempered, more forgiving, and easygoing. They are a powerful force for peace on the planet. They are able to accomplish their goals of peace and unity mostly because the Indigos led the way before them, cutting down and challenging anything that lacked integrity.

# Treasures of the Soul

I am Allison Drusilla Mainer. I was born October 4, 1990. Although, I now understand that I am an Indigo child, I did not for most of my childhood. I was misunderstood by my family and myself. I was considered uncontrollable, difficult, violent, and unstable. I was, at times, all of these things and more. Yet, I always, always could see a larger vision of how people and the whole world should be. I hated when people lied to me, and I always knew. I couldn't stand it when I saw someone who did not live up to his or her potential, and I pushed and pushed trying to make them see that my vision was right and theirs was wrong. This usually didn't— no actually—never worked very well for me. When someone was being unjustly treated, even if it was someone I didn't like, I stood up for them, simply because to do otherwise went against my basic nature and instinct.

I have thought a lot about my childhood and why I behaved the way I did. My mom taught me to be peaceful, kind, and forgiving. My dad taught me that the world could be a dangerous place, and I would be wise not to trust anyone too easily. He would tell me that life was a game to fight and to win—no matter what. My mom and dad were two very different people. They seemed to be complete opposites, and the constant tension between them was upsetting to me. I wanted to find my own way of being. I seemed to vacillate between anger and fear, believing that trust and surrender would lead to lack of control, and defeat.

I knew in my heart there was an answer, and I was determined to find it. My behavior, however, became outrageous, and my inability to control my anxiety led me into therapy and a diagnosis of "possible" borderline personality disorder or bipolar disorder. I refused to believe either of them and refused to believe that medication was the answer to my problems. Unfortunately, many Indigo children are medicated because they are so misunderstood. As a result, they lose their beautiful sensitivity, warrior energy, and spiritual gifts. I think, somehow, I was aware of this. A psychiatrist I was seeing once read me the characteristics of borderline personality disorder in an attempt to convince me that was my problem, and I needed medication right away.

"I hear you," I responded. "I agree that some of what you read to me fits my personality today. However, I am only fifteen years old, and I refuse to define myself at this age. I have issues. Who wouldn't with all I have been through? I believe that I can change who I am and become who I want to be by changing what I think about and how I see the world. If you give me medication, I will never know whether who I become will be due to the drugs you prescribe, or from digging down deep inside of me, overcoming my issues and being the best I can be."

My mom was a bit stunned by my answer. The psychiatrist, still urging drug therapy, looked at my mom. Mom looked into my eyes, smiled and took my hand. She then looked directly at the doctor.

"No drugs, I believe in her," she said. "I think she deserves my faith and the chance to find a way to heal that feels right for her. She is and has always been strong, wise, and insightful. Let's let her try."

My mom has always stood by me no matter what I did, and believe me; some of the things were pretty bad.

I guess the best way to describe what it was like in my internal world is an environment of low frustration and high anxiety. Everyone, at times, feels overwhelmed and ready to "melt down" at the smallest thing. Well imagine feeling that way all the time. That was me. Sometimes, something would happen at school that upset me. My anxiety would begin to rise and I couldn't control it. I felt like I was on the edge of a cliff and something was urging me, pushing me to jump. I couldn't. I had to wait until I got home because if I jumped, there would be no one to catch me. That no one, of course, was my mom. So I clung to the branches of a tree at the cliff's edge, my knuckles white with tension, my skin crawling, and my heart racing. I couldn't breathe. After a while I didn't even remember why I was upset. I just needed to release the pain—let go. I needed to get home.

Finally, I walked in the door of our home and that's when the turmoil began. I started to fight with everyone. I argued with my brother and sister. Brianne usually ignored me but I could push Jake's buttons and sometimes we came to blows. I needed, I mean I really needed to get everyone upset, because for reasons I didn't understand, and still don't, it made me feel better. After a while they both retreated to their rooms. Then Mom would come home from work and it was her turn. I would "get in her face," puff myself up to mask the fear and the craziness I was feeling inside. She tried to stay calm and rational … tried to help me calm down and find answers. I didn't want answers then, not then … I wanted her to enter my pain … come inside of me … feel it with me. I wanted her to cry the tears I couldn't cry because I was too afraid to feel vulnerable. I knew she had that vulnerability inside of her and I needed to bring it out. God, I still really don't know exactly why. These episodes would sometimes go on for hours until my mom couldn't handle it anymore, and she would finally collapse in frustration and heartache, tears flowing. When this happened I felt an odd, emotional release, and then it could finally be over.

It wasn't really over, though. There was always the next time. Eventually, my mom stopped trusting me. She became afraid of my moods. Many times she just pushed me away hoping to avoid another emotional ordeal. I couldn't blame her. Yet, I knew, that in the very deepest part of me, she loved me so completely and unconditionally, that she would never leave me. She would never abandon me. She would never give up on me. So I had to work harder. I had to overcome my "demons" for me, and my family. I needed their love and support. I needed their friendship and trust. I knew I wanted to do great things with my life. I did a tremendous amount of inner work. I read books and listened to self-help tapes about loving myself more. I went to counseling every week with my mom. We cried together, we laughed, and we grew, sometimes closer—sometimes farther apart. We had setbacks and then we surged forward until eventually I started to remember my true Indigo essence.

I am an Indigo child. I have huge almond shaped blue eyes and long blond hair. I have a fiery temper that I now reserve for battles against injustice, and things I believe should change—at least most of the time. I am a warrior for peace and fairness. I believe in a brighter vision for our world, and for me. I am in college now and studying neuroscience. I'm not sure exactly where it will lead me, but I trust my spirit to show me my path and my life's purpose. I am an Indigo child who was raised by a *light worker*, a woman who was aware that beneath my pain and confusion, was a bright and gifted soul. I am grateful. I am an Indigo child who is now a young Indigo woman. I continue to search and to struggle, as we all do, but today I remember—I am an Indigo child!

"UNCONDITIONAL LOVE
IS A CHOICE.
ONCE THAT CHOICE IS MADE
NOTHING CAN DESTROY IT,
AND ITS INCREASING POWER
CAN TRANSFORM DARKNESS
INTO LIGHT AND CHAOS INTO PEACE.
BRAVO ALLISON!"

# What Lies Beneath

*(Words of encouragement for Allison)*

You turn to me for strength, my child;
How I want you to succeed—
So hard to see you struggling,
Birthing dreams from tiny seeds.

My faith is like a massive oak
Faltering not, amidst your pain.
For rainbows always follow your storms
Thrusting doubt from whence it came.

Remember, Allison, how far you've come
From those years of turmoil and strife;
You planted your soulful seeds of faith
In Heaven's soil, the source of life.

That soil, so rich in hopes and dreams
Assures gardens full of greatness and light.
Envision beneath the surface's crust
Seeds ascending in the darkness of night.

Your trust, my daughter, is the food they need
To continue their journey to this world
With perseverance and much self-love.
They burst forth and their petals unfurl.

When you feel your path is too much to bear,
Be mindful of those souls you'll assist.
Steadfast, hold visions of hope for them all;
Thoughts of failure, you must resist.

I offer these words from a mother's heart
Knowing you soar on angels' wings.
God called your soul, you vowed to serve
Facing bravely whatever life brings.

So take my hand, my heart, and my love
Pressing forth on your mission in this sphere.
Yet, rely on God, your angels, and your sight
To build faith, and let go of fear.

I believe in you, Ali, forever I will,
Not because my seed gave you life;
You inspire, encourage, and believe in the good
Leaving me smiling with pride and delight.

As a mother, I have found that
I never have all the answers.
However, the one thing
that is my greatest tool
and my assurance
that I am doing my best
is unconditional love,
no matter what."

# A Mother's Tribute

*(Brianne and Allison, both off to college)*

A distant time not long ago
You resided in my womb.
Your tiny forms took sturdy roots—
Your souls, they thrived and they bloomed.

Then, one day your spirits burst forth,
Your hearts and eyes how they shined.
Tears of joy and dreams of your future
Continued to flow through time.

Falls, winters, summers, and springs
Passed quickly, or so it seemed—
Christmas trees, flowers and rain,
Snowflakes, pumpkins, and streams.

Your angels carried you through the rivers of life
So much filled with turmoil and strife,
But my brave sweet babies so strong and bright
Were amazing as you always cherished life.

You danced, and dreamed, and charted your course
Determined to make your mark.
I prayed, and encouraged, and dreamed with you, too
As you made plans that would move us apart.

The final summer of these times now ends.
You are both gone, and settled, and free.
Your dreams are unfolding as we hoped they would,
Yet my heart feels so empty and I weep.

My tears are confusing for I am so proud of you both.
You've overcome things no child should endure;
You rose above adversity, violence, and abuse,
Knowing better choices were the only cure.

And so my young daughters this tribute is to you—
My heroes, my inspiration, my pride.
My blessings and my love will keep you both safe;
My spirit will, forever, be by your side.

"I AM CONSISTENTLY REMINDED
THAT, THOUGH I GAVE BIRTH TO MY
CHILDREN, THEY ARE INDIVIDUAL,
WISE, AND ENLIGHTENED SOULS THAT
HAVE AS MUCH TO TEACH ME AS I
HAVE TO TEACH THEM.
I AM, AND WILL ALWAYS BE GRATEFUL
FOR THEIR PRESENCE IN MY LIFE,
AND THE LOVE THAT WE SHARE."

# No Ordinary Days

"*T*ime to get up, sleepyhead," whispered my trusted and dependable biological alarm clock ever so softly into my ear. "It's 5:30 a.m."

"Oh no, please not yet," I silently pleaded.

The night had yielded the deepest, dreamiest slumber—the kind that leaves you feeling as if you've been held safely in the nurturing arms of Divinity. Sweet memories of timeless cosmic journeys to places beyond this world filled my waking mind. I begged time to stand still so I could return to that ethereal space that always offers me visions of my immortal past, answers to my probing questions about life's mysteries, as well as my own enigmas and mystical purpose in this earthly realm.

I feel another soft nudge within the silence of my consciousness, and I slowly roll into a sitting position rubbing the angel dust from my eyes and willing myself to rise. I have to get to the lab by 6:00 a.m. to have blood drawn. The cardiologist wants to check my cholesterol despite the fact that the EKG, Stress Test, and Echocardiogram all turned out to be normal, thank God. Sam's recent open heart surgery has shaken me deeply and caused me to feel uneasy about my own heart health. I have a history of heart disease in my family, so I decided to make sure I was OK. Even though Sam did amazingly well after *his* surgery, it was a horrendous ordeal, and I vowed to do everything I possibly could to avoid that suffering for myself.

In the darkness, I grab the clothes I had laid out the night before. I quietly make my way to the bathroom trying not to wake Sam. Still semiconscious, due to my resistance in releasing the night's embrace, I slip into autopilot and now find myself sitting behind the wheel of my car.

"OK, Dru," commands my highly agitated left-brain-self who is anxious to get on with the task at hand. "Snap out of it. You need to have all of your senses in working order right now."

I try to shake the final wisps of blissful, dreamy fog from my head, turn on the car lights and back out of the driveway. I turn left onto the main road.

"Wow, look at that moon," I declare to myself. "It is so full, so bright, and so unbelievably beautiful."

I find it hard to keep my eyes on the road. No matter how many times I have gazed in awe at a gloriously and perfectly symmetrical full moon, there is always something about that translucent, living, vital orb that draws me deeply into its luminescent core. Perhaps, it is the heavenly memories of my soul's time spent in between earthly incarnations surrounded and embraced by the brilliant divine light and the infinite glory of God's eternal Love. Yes, that's what it must be! Our amazing Creator fashioned a myriad of celestial entities like the sun, moon, and stars to spark a memory of what it is like to be in His presence—to be connected to Him, an extension of Him—to know without uncertainty or doubt what it means to "be" the light of love, goodness and true, and everlasting peace.

I pull into the parking lot discreetly tucked away behind a shopping center. There is not a soul around and no cars in the lot except for mine. Every building is dark, and there is no outside lighting. It is an eerie, uncomfortable feeling. I wonder if I have gotten the hours of the lab wrong. The small fearful child begins to emerge urging me to leave this place at once because it is too scary. However, by now I know the distinct difference between my frightened ego-self and my calm spiritual guidance. I know with certainty that the voice is clearly my ego and not my guides or angels. So I turn into a parking space directly in front of the lab and turn off my headlights. The moon, shimmering like an enormous shiny pearl, is now an inspired backdrop hanging spectacularly low over the Western sky. Hints of twilight and the first sprays of morning sunlight beckon alluringly in the East. It is a perfect time to go within and connect to that space inside of me wherein lie, truth, inspiration, and enlightenment.

I close my eyes, focusing on my sixth chakra, the space between my two physical eyes, sometimes called the "seat of the soul." I wait patiently for images or messages to pass through the ethereal mist into my receptive mind. I feel peaceful and relaxed. In the darkness of my inner world, I rest, poised with anticipation on a sacred bridge composed of pure energy and light, linking one reality to the other.

"Each day is, in and of itself, an entire lifetime," begins the familiar, calm and steady voice of my spirit guide who delivers his messages with a cadence and rhythm that is filled with strength, clarity, and truth. "Too often, you feel as if living fully as your higher self for merely one day and journeying steadily on your destined path for that time, is miniscule in the largeness of your whole life. I say to you, however, that in spirit time is an endless 'Now.' Each and every day is a chance to begin anew, to live sunrise to sunset as if it were from birth until death. As you arise, you are born likening yourself to an infant child. The life before you is pregnant with possibility. At midday you embrace the height of youth and activity. You are strong, vital, and feel capable of greatness. You are certain that you can face and conquer any and all challenges that lie on your path. As darkness approaches you feel weary. You pull back and slow down. At this time, it is wise to reflect on the day—the life that you have just lived—no regrets, only gratitude for experiences offered and lessons learned, or perhaps not learned. Then you rest in the world of spirit in your dreams, processing all that your previous life presented to you—how you responded or how you possibly could have responded differently—

journeying, floating, contemplating, until you are born once again with the rising of the morning sun."

Suddenly the glare of headlights from behind pulls me back to the physical and back to the task at hand, my blood test. Not many people venture out quite so early, so I am in and out in about fifteen minutes. As I leave the lab, the sun is now steadily ascending, illuminating, and reflecting what little color exists on this rather dreary March day. I look up at the barren tree branches as I make my way back to our home. I am still feeling a little lightheaded and foggy, when suddenly—unexpected visions of the first buds of spring seem to magically appear on the lifeless vegetation. As I step out of my car I hear a glorious sound—birds, lots and lots of birds chirping, singing, and excitedly announcing the arrival of that incredible forthcoming season of rebirth and renewal. I feel excited and joyful as I walk slowly into the house ready and motivated to begin my new day—my new life.

"I WILL TRY TO LIVE EACH DAY
FULLY, ACTIVELY AND PEACEFULLY AS
IF IT WERE AN ENTIRE LIFE.
I WILL DREAM MY DREAMS AND SET
MY GOALS AS IF MY PRESENT LIFE
HAD NO BEGINNING AND NO END.
I WILL DO MY BEST
TO STAY FULLY GROUNDED IN
THE TIMELESSNESS OF THE 'NOW.'"

# *Grief Buried Alive Finds a Way*

*I* sit quietly in the small bistro room in the back of our house, gazing out the large bay window adorned with plants. I am finally beginning to regain some tranquility and peace that was completely unavailable to me yesterday. It is early morning. A light coating of fluffy crystal-like snow clings to the barren branches, and blankets the cold, sleeping earth. He died last night at 8:35 p.m., January 18, 2009. My ex-father in law, Jake, left this physical world in a moment that I believe was in complete surrender and peace. He seemed to know it was his time, but patiently waited until his family was ready to let him go—at least as ready as they could be.

He wasn't a very spiritual man, as far as I knew. He went to church, though. I think he did so out of a sense of duty or perhaps at the urging of his wife of many years, Arlene. His final days were spent in the hospital. Those hours were filled with doctors, tests, kidney dialysis, and the endless repetition of everyone asking him how he felt. Eventually his response to all their concerned questions, I was told, was simple, "God will take care of me."

My daughters—his grandchildren—saw this as a sign that he was giving up and had stopped fighting. In the weeks leading up to his death, my children struggled to accept what was happening. They had never experienced death before. They were sad, feeling helpless, and worried about their grandma and their dad. I tried to explain to them that grandpa was in a space between two worlds. He was beginning to move, beginning to release the physical form that housed his soul and was about to return home to the world of spirit. I told them that death was just an illusion and

214

that none of us really ever dies, for our souls are eternal and everlasting. We talked about the fact that he was so very ill, on oxygen twenty-four hours a day. His kidneys had failed and dialysis was no longer prolonging his life—it was prolonging his death.

"Grandpa would never want to live in this state of merely existing," I explained trying to comfort them.

He had always been so vital and active. I remember him spending endless hours in his gardens, and he was always fixing and building things. He loved life, was always on the move, and now he couldn't move. He could hardly breathe. He was ready to move on. In my prayers I asked God to surround him with angels and fill him with faith, joy, and a sense of completion. I asked that one of my angels be present when he passed so that he would know that my heart was with him. I seemed to be handling his passing as if it were as natural as breathing, as predictable as the dawn that always follows even the darkest night, and as if it were just another dream that would eventually awaken to another day.

Yesterday it became clear that his last breath was imminent. Without warning and taking me completely by surprise, a flood of unresolved sadness and grief spilled forth from my heart. I had loved him. I had called him "Dad." Then one day, overnight, he left my life. He never said goodbye. He merely stopped speaking to me. That was thirteen years ago. He had known about the problems between Jake and me, and had comforted me. When I finally had enough and decided to leave my marriage, however, that was the end of my relationship with my father-in-law too. The divorce, it seemed, required taking sides and so he and my mother-in-law did, and I was out of their lives forever. I guess I understood, somewhat, at the time. He was their son. They thought they had no choice and needed to support him. However, I was awfully hurt and felt terribly abandoned. That hurt was quickly brushed aside. There were too many other things to deal with. I was fighting for my life and for custody of my kids. I was in school full time. Once that was over, I had three children to raise, a job to find, bills to pay, and I had to find a place to live. The sadness and grief over the loss of my second Mom and Dad would have to wait. It did wait until yesterday, when the finality of that loss slashed into my heart and opened up a wound that had been sealed tight by the hardened tissue of my unforgotten pain. Tears and heartache erupted like a volcano that could no longer contain the pressure deep within its walls. The only thing to do was to wait until the seemingly endless lava of sorrowful tears had run its course.

I grieved alone yesterday. There was no one with whom to share my aching heart. I will not be part of "the saying goodbye." It is not my place. My daughters are dealing with their own pain and don't really understand why his death has affected me so deeply. They don't remember my relationship with their grandpa. I wonder about it, as well, since it has been so many years since I have seen him, but the truth is that his death has truly affected me deeply. I wanted intensely to go to the wake and funeral but I thought my presence would create discomfort for everyone.

So yesterday, I cried my silent tears and not so silent tears. I spoke softly to him of all the things I never got a chance to say when he was here, and I felt comforted knowing he could hear me. There was now no physical space separating us and my thoughts alone could tell him that I had never stopped loving him. I would always love him. Looking out once again at the beginning of this new January day, cold, grey, and lifeless, I say my final goodbye to "Dad." A few tears still linger but they fall softly and gently like a slow moving stream meandering through a beautiful, sun-soaked countryside. Tranquility has replaced the anguish, and I smile as I imagine him planting magnificent gardens in heaven's lush, rich soil.

Enjoy your journey, Dad, until we meet again.

> "ALL FEELINGS,
> IF WE BURY THEM ALIVE,
> WILL NEVER REALLY DIE.
> THEY LAY JUST BENEATH THE
> SURFACE OF OUR CONSCIOUSNESS
> WAITING FOR THE MOMENT WHEN
> THEY CAN BE RELEASED
> AND OUR PAIN CAN BE HEALED."

# Sweet Brianne

*(Brianne Graduates from College)*

So many years have come and gone
Since I first held you in my arms …
So many moments on bended knee,
Praying, "God keep her safe from harm."

You entered this world with angel's wings,
Spoke softly, and cried few tears.
Surrounded by chaos, violence, and pain
You stayed focused to calm your fears.

Loyalty, honor, love, and truth
Were the qualities that rose from your core.
Your family and friends were drawn to your peace;
Your pure heart made us love you more.

You set your goals determined to succeed
Despite obstacles no child should endure.
Slow and steady, consistent and strong,
You climbed mountains and opened each door.

From high school to college you surged ahead
Working tirelessly as you reached for your dreams.
Excellence was the bar that you set for your life
And nothing was beyond your means.

Today my sweet Bri, my daughter, my heart,
You stand beautiful, regal, and proud
Wearing robes of purple and celestial gold—
They call your name and distinction out loud.

Magna Cum Laude is heard through the crowd
As a tidal wave of tears is unleashed.
Memories of your journey flash through my mind
And a rainbow of emotions is released.

I'd like to take credit but this moment is yours;
I'm so proud of my sweet baby girl.
From toddler to teen to the young woman you are,
Life polishes you like a developing pearl.

So here's to you, Bri, my inspiration, my friend:
I wish you happiness, adventure, and fun;
May your laughter be abundant and your sorrows few;
May love warm you like the rays of the sun.

**"OUR CHILDREN ARE ENTRUSTED TO US.
WE LOVE THEM, GUIDE THEM
AND INSPIRE THEM AND THEN,
ONE DAY, THEY MIRACULOUSLY
DO THE SAME FOR US."**

# Sacred Contract

*T*he lush, green canopy of midsummer thins daily revealing more and more of the bony, skeletal arms that annually accept with reverence, the impending icy, stillness of winter. October's chill has a rigid, unrelenting grip, and the crisp, autumn breezes prepare my heart and mind for the beginning of yet, another inevitable death and rebirth.

As always, this time of year creates a resurgence of uneasiness with all things physical. The resounding call of my soul urges me to release the illusions of what can be seen by my single dimensional personality and look beyond into the world of spirit, engaging my multidimensional self and gifts of clairaudience (clear hearing), clairsentience (clear sensing), and occasionally clairvoyance (clear seeing).

I wonder continuously, and at times painstakingly, at the non-coincidences that occur daily that have occurred throughout my life thus far. I regularly and ritualistically rise above the arena of my current incarnation and try to view it from a higher, more spiritual perspective. I observe each of the co-participants in my personal drama and attempt to converse with them on a subconscious, nonphysical level in an effort to gain clarity and truth about our purpose in each other's lives.

One of the most telling and controversial of those exchanges occurred between me and my ex-husband, Jake. During this self-initiated soul to soul conversation with him, I found myself transported to a great ethereal hall called "The Hall of Transitions." This otherworldly place exists in the "life-between-life" state, where along with my guides and my council of elders, I believe that I planned my present incarnation. It was a time of great decision making.

"What lessons will I choose to learn? What experiences and adversities will I create to help me awaken and remember my divine self? Who in my Soul Group or another will agree to form a sacred contract with me in order to help me accomplish my goals and life purpose?"

I am shown various possibilities that I view on a large panoramic screen. I must make very specific choices that will be significant in initiating my awakening.

"In what part of the world will I be born and grow up? What parents would be best suited for me? What body, with all of its biological and chemical components would provide the best vehicle and personality through which my soul could express itself?"

One by one, members of my current family, my friends, and even my remote acquaintances agree to share my journey, as I agree to share theirs. The process of accomplishing the necessary synchronicities seems intensely complicated and yet extremely simple at the same time. I am able to view many future life experiences as well as the possible choices that will be presented to me throughout my life. Choosing wisely will determine my success in following my predetermined path.

It is now time to choose a mate. I see the soul of my first husband Jake move toward me, as I have asked him to come. I am aware that my greatest challenge in the next lifetime will be to truly embrace and embody self-love. I will endeavor to remember that I am a powerful being of light, devoted to the task of radiating and anchoring more of that Divine Love into Human Consciousness. In past incarnations I have fallen short, allowing fear and self-doubt to obscure my personal truth. Understanding that as human beings we learn best through contrast, I know that I must face and conquer this challenge once and for all. I will be required to confront my longing for that self-love by being married to someone who

221

could not fill the void. Through my sense of isolation and despair, and with no answers externally, I will be forced to go to a place deep within. I must remember that looking for love outside of myself in order to feel complete, will never bring lasting joy and peace. By contrast, discovering the spark of Divine Love within me—my soul—I will finally know self-love.

"I am asking you, the soul who will be Jake, to play this difficult role for me in my next life. I need you to agree to take on the task of being my husband and take a journey with me that will not be easy, and one that will eventually end badly. This is necessary so that I can fully awaken in my next lifetime and remember myself as a soul consisting only of love, and one who experiences my humanity fully and completely."

"I cannot," he responds adamantly. "My love for your soul prevents this. I do not wish to hurt you."

"I understand," I reply with compassion. "However, it is important. Your sacred contract with me is necessary. I agree to it fully, knowing you will not incur any negative karma through your participation. You are already forgiven for all that may happen."

The soul of Jake eventually agrees, our contract is sealed, and I return to my present moment on the earth plane.

Through the filter of my human brain, I contemplate this possibility. While in an altered state, this scenario seemed reasonable and logical. Now, however, I wonder as images of our life together—the intense pain I experienced during my relationship with him—fill my consciousness. Yet, the idea of this being potentially true transmutes my dark memories of hurt and suffering into a soft, gentle, enveloping mist of necessity and completion. I am reminded of the fact that I never once believed that Jake didn't love me despite actions that may times suggested otherwise. Forgiving him was never a struggle for me, as well, no matter what he did or said. Forgiveness was as easy as accepting my next breath, natural and unconscious. I never questioned whether or not to forgive. For me, it was the only choice. I gave it freely and most of the time, without expectation or attachment to the outcome.

It is and has always been far easier for me to believe in goodness than not. Therefore, I will reach no conclusion, as of yet, regarding this appealing perspective. I will choose to believe in the divine light of love that is the soul of Jake. I will offer him my deepest gratitude for assisting in my awakening, and will extend to him a prayer that he may also find the peace and remembrance of his own sacred contracts. I pray for his own awakening and that he will live the remainder of his life in Love and Gratitude.

> "MANY OF LIFE'S MYSTERIES HAVE NO CLEAR ANSWERS. IN THE FACE OF THE UNKNOWN OR EVEN A VIEW THAT SEEMS DISTORTED AND CONFUSING, I WILL CHOOSE THE PATH OF LOVE. THAT ONE WORD CAN SIMPLIFY EVEN THE MOST COMPLICATED EXPERIENCES. EVENTUALLY, IN TIME, THE TRUTH WILL BE REVEALED."

# My Mom, A Gift of Love and Light

Closing my eyes I journey
Back in time, spanning fifty years
When her "summer" is just beginning;
Her youth blooms despite a childhood of tears.

Sunlight filters through the open blinds.
She prepares for another day:
Breakfast, lunches, so much to do—
Eight children, no time to play.

Her face is gentle, soft, and kind—
Her voice, like a beautiful song.
She treats each one of us with tenderness and love,
Even when we've done something wrong.

She moves like a swan, graceful and strong,
Never angry, harsh, or mean.
She teaches us to face the world with hope;
She insists that her family is a team.

"The only thing I ask," she implores us,
"Is to love each other with all your hearts;
You may not always agree on things
But don't let anything pull you apart."

I open my eyes and I see her.
Years have passed, and she is old.
Yet, her face is still soft and gentle;
Time has not altered her soul.

She pushes her walker across the floor
Moving her legs is a constant fight.
She doesn't notice the tears in my eyes;
Being so crippled ... it just isn't right.

"It's alright," she responds to my silence.
"I have much to be grateful for.
Each night I thank God for my blessings;
Before I can finish, I walk through sleep's door."

We listened to my mom, my siblings and me.
We don't fight because she asked us to love.
That bond she created is genuine and strong
Any differences—we always rise above.

Our family has grown from a few to so many.
We continue the legacy she began.
We teach our children to always choose love
And forgiveness whenever they can.

"We love you Mom, grandmother, Jean.
You are our inspiration, our beacon in the night.
If we need to remember how beautiful life is,
We think of you … our gift of love and light"

"MOM TAUGHT US MANY THINGS.
HOWEVER,
THE MOST IMPORTANT THING
I LEARNED FROM HER WAS
THAT WHEN IT COMES TO FAMILY;
LOVE, FORGIVENESS, AND LETTING GO
OF PETTY DIFFERENCES ARE CHOICES
THAT MUST BE MADE,
NO MATTER WHAT!
MY BROTHERS, MY SISTERS, AND I
ALL LOVE EACH OTHER
FOR MANY REASONS,
MOST IMPORTANTLY BECAUSE
'MOM SAID SO.'"

# *Seeing what is Said*

*T*he lights were already out. My older sister Susan and my younger sister Sara were sharing the spare bedroom at my mom's house in Florida. The year was 2004 when we had a most memorable girl's weekend with just my mom and her six daughters. Sara realized she needed to tell Sue something before they went to sleep. Knowing that Susan is hearing impaired, she also knew Sue would need light to be able to read Sara's lips to "see what she was saying."

"Sue, turn on the light for a sec, I need to tell you something."

"What, Sara, I didn't get that. Could you repeat it?"

"Turn on the light so you can hear me!"

"What, I still didn't understand."

"Oh my God," shouted Sara, now utterly frustrated. "Turn on the freakin' light."

"Hang on a second, Sara," Sue said softly. "Let me turn on the light so I can see what you're saying."

After telling Sue whatever it was she needed, she then repeated the hilarious conversation that had just transpired and they both laughed until they cried—so did the rest of us for the entire weekend.

This is a pretty amusing story, no doubt. However, being hearing impaired, as I am also, is not easy. Though I wear a hearing aid, it is not the same as putting on glasses to correct your eyesight. They help, but you never get 100% of a conversation, all of the words spoken while watching a movie, or everything a professor says during a lecture. It's difficult for people with normal hearing to understand what it's like, unless they've grown up with someone who has a hearing disability. Someone who doesn't know me well may sometimes think I am being rude if I don't answer them when they speak to me. They may believe either I'm ignoring them, or I am a snob. Sometimes people think I am mentally slow or just plain stupid. Oftentimes, they get a good, hearty laugh when I hear something differently from what was said, and respond accordingly.

Here's an example:

"Hey Dru, are you coming to the movies tonight?"

"I know, I know, these jeans are a little too tight."

The only thing I heard, of course, was the "ight" at the end, and my mind incorrectly filled in the rest. Most of the time, I can laugh along with them. But, at other times, it takes everything I have not to break down in tears from the humiliation and embarrassment I feel.

Sam and I love going to his sister Tori's lake house. It is a magnificent playground with lots of water toys like a pontoon boat, a speed boat, and a couple of jet skis, not to mention lots of good food, drinks, and great company. One of the things Tori loves to do is have a big bonfire right by the edge of the lake just as the sun is beginning to set. We all grab a chair and gather around the fire, drink in hand; we talk, tell jokes, and enjoy the incredible backdrop of the beautiful lake.

At first, when there's still a little light from the evening sun as it begins its decent beneath the horizon, I can almost keep up with the conversations. However, as that bright blazing orb disappears, and darkness envelops us, not even a brilliant full moon on a clear, starry, night can help me. I hear laughter and voices but have no idea what's being said. I smile trying to appear as if I am part of the festivities. The truth is, however, that I feel more and more alone, and isolated in my own silent world as the evening progresses. I struggle with my thoughts, feelings of sadness, and loneliness. I try to enjoy myself anyway and remind myself that this is my life, remember all the blessings I have, and also that I could have a lot worse wrong with me than just hearing loss. This, honestly, is how I think and feel about my disability most of the time. Situations like this are difficult, though. So eventually, I retreat to the house where I can enjoy my own company by reading a good book or simply calling it a night, and unfortunately, leaving some people wondering if I'm OK or if something is wrong.

It's not all bad, though. Being hearing impaired has its benefits. When my kids were little, fighting, or merely being normal kids raising the sound levels in our home to unbearable decibels, I yanked that tiny microphone from my ear and voiced a silent *ahhhhh,* as I returned to my quiet, peaceful place.

As I do with most adversity in my life, I try to find the positive and determine how it has helped me. Because I wasn't always able to be fully engaged in the outside world, I retreated into my rich, mystical and magical world within. This allowed me to journey on an amazing, transformational, spiritual path. Through it, I remembered the purpose, for which I chose to come here. I remembered my authentic divine self and my beautiful loving spirit. I truly learned to love myself. Choosing this disability before I incarnated, which I believe I did, was done for a very good reason—to help me accomplish my goals and recall all I promised to do on earth. So I embrace all of my life, even my hearing loss, and I always try to find humor in the crazy things that happen as a result of it.

"Sam, it's late. It's been a great New Year's Eve, but I'm tired. I think I'll go to bed," I said as I yawned, lifted my weary body from the couch, and headed for the bathroom.

After removing my hearing aid, washing my face and brushing my teeth, I went into the bedroom anticipating my nice soft flannel sheets, and warm, comfy blanket. Sam was sitting on the edge of the bed and motioned for me to sit next to him. He looked serious and focused—maybe even a little nervous—so I figured that whatever he needed to tell me was important.

"Dru, he said softly …"

"What?" I questioned after he had spoken a few sentences. I was hoping I'd catch on to what he was saying, which I can do sometimes. "I'm having some trouble hearing you."

Sam tried a few more times, raising his voice a little more each time, and I continued to ask him to repeat himself. I could tell he was becoming more and more visibly frustrated.

"Hang on a second," I finally said. "Let me put my hearing aid in so I can hear you better."

He began again for the—I don't know what numbered time—, and it was then I realized what was happening. Sam was asking me to marry him. He had a beautiful poetic speech all planned. It didn't go exactly the way he had hoped, and I was so embarrassed. I had pretty much rewritten the fairy tale moment he was trying to give me into a bizarre comedy. Of course, I was thrilled, and I absolutely said yes to the man of my dreams. We still laugh about it and especially when people ask how he proposed. It makes for a great story that we can pass down to our kids and grandkids.

We all have something that challenges us when it comes to taking on the human form. Maybe it's our big nose, overly pudgy thighs, or chronic asthma. Maybe we think we're too fat, too thin, too short, or too tall. The one thing we know for sure is, though the soul is perfect, no one's body is truly perfect. I am grateful, most of the time, for the lessons I continue to learn from this disability, and the new ways I am able to adapt as my hearing worsens with age. I see my mom, who is legally deaf, and

I know what might be in store for me. I also watch her, however, being proactive, taking advantage of all the new devices and gadgets for the hearing impaired that keep her in "the game of life." She inspires me with her consistent attitude of gratitude. I hope in sharing this story that people might be a little bit more compassionate, patient, and sensitive when trying to communicate with a hearing impaired person. Face them directly so they can see your lips, speak clearly and slowly—not necessarily more loudly. Articulate carefully by forming words in a little more exaggerated manner and please, please, please don't roll your eyes and sigh deeply when they say "what" for the third time. We will all appreciate it more than you could ever know.

> "OUR AFFLICTIONS CAN BE
> AMAZINGLY TRANSFORMATIONAL
> AND ENLIGHTENING
> IF WE EMBRACE THEM
> WITH GRATITUDE
> WHILE, AT THE SAME TIME,
> WE SEARCH FOR SOLUTIONS
> TO OVERCOME THEM OR
> THE COURAGE TO ACCEPT THEM."

# The Illusion of Time

"*I* can't believe our vacation is over already," I muse pensively.

It was wonderful to see everyone at our family reunion in Saint Augustine, Florida. We rented a total of eight condominiums in a beautiful resort called Ocean Gardens. Most of the units had sliding glass doors that opened up to a majestic, panoramic view of the Atlantic Ocean. Going to sleep and waking up to the rhythmic, gentle, tumbling, or violent, turbulent, pounding of the surf was intoxicating. Sunrises on our deck, as the Eastern sky gave birth to that brilliant, fiery globe, were magnificent and breathtaking creating an amber glow that shined upon the surface of the sea reflecting back crystals of orange and red ethereal light. Coffee never tasted so good! Our days were spent divided between lounging at the pool, talking quietly, and tossing squish balls with kids—then taking a short walk on the boardwalk to the beach where we frolicked in the surf, went kayaking, and played "corn hole" among other games. Each night we gathered at around five or six o'clock at a different condo, bringing a favorite gourmet delicacy and our drink of choice. We enjoyed happy hours—to top all happy hours—that lasted into the night. The jokes, belly laughs, stories, and shared memories of our lives together made for a great time for all. Burroughs sure know how to have fun!

As I reflect back on the past week, however, I begin to move more deeply into the dynamics and personal intricacies that became woven like a colorful tapestry throughout the week's adventures. With all those people and so many different ages, personalities, and unique family differences, it got complicated at times.

We, my siblings and I, all have our own lives now, and have for quite some time. We mapped out those lives over time and we have traveled our paths paved with years of growth and change. We reside in our own personal "countries," with boundaries defined and determined by individual laws and codes of conduct, as well as the self-created "culture" formed through combinations of each of the members our families. When we come together, it is as if we are somewhere in between that sacred space and a multi-memory childhood depending on whose memory is being explored. It is a sort of twilight zone, if you will, with hints of the adult present and confusion from a childhood past. All the old issues arise; "pain bodies" sometimes wake up causing emotional, and for me, physical pain. Sibling order bounces back as the younger ones feel invalidated, or viewed once again, as the "little ones." Subconsciously jockeying for position, each of our voices of reason and clarity tries unassumingly to be heard. This leaves everyone talking a little louder; and contributing to the rise in decibel levels is that half of us is hearing impaired. Then there are the little and not so little dramas being played out as small groups of middle-aged bathing beauties and grey-haired studs try to determine the appropriate outcome—who is the victim and perpetrator in the over-dramatized scenarios.

It sounds like a lot of gossip, right? It is. However, permeating throughout countless hours of whispered "hashing over" the moment to moment unfolding is boundless love and unshakable family commitment. Acknowledging, individually, that we all have our own painful issues, each of us believes we are trying to help and have the answers, having overcome certain adversities ourselves. Some of us are grateful not to be the one who is the focus of Burrough scrutiny; and others, though uncomfortable, are happy to be able to share with and be supported by those people in our lives that love us the most—family. Tears flow off and on as sisters and brothers, who haven't shared intimate moments in far too long, renew or reshape precious and lasting bonds. Cousins, who don't see each other often, form new friendships and connections we all hope will continue beyond this one encounter. Just being all together after ten years is a gift treasured by all, knowing that it will probably be quite some time before it is experienced again.

Mom is in her twilight years. The winter of her life displays a time of little physical activity or growth—merely a quiet peacefulness. Her mind, though, is sharp as ever, and her spirit kind and loving as always. We all try to wrap our minds around the fact that Mommy will not be with us forever, and each day leaves her more and more dependent on her children. Yet, we still learn from her as she faces her challenges with a gentle smile and calm acceptance, at the same time trying to remain fully engaged in life. That can be challenging. She remains focused on only what is good in her life. Through our time together, I think we came to realize how much my brothers Mike and Charlie, and now my sister Sara and their families, do for her on a daily basis because they are in Florida with her. Thank God they are who they are and are consistently there for her. I am grateful.

As this crazy, chaotic time comes to a close, we say our goodbyes. This moment goes on and on as we make sure we don't leave anyone out. Hugging and kissing with tears of joy for the time spent and sadness for having it end, we bump into and maneuver around, the thirty-something present members of our beautiful family—a family that emerged from two people, both without siblings, falling in love. It is quite a sight. Eventually the room empties, and we all prepare to head back home taking with us incredible memories that must last until the next time, hopefully not another ten years.

It is 6:00 a.m. Sitting outside, once again, on our patio in my place of solitude and natural beauty, I am overwhelmed with emotion. The source of my free-flowing tears is a mystery to me beckoning to be solved. I am glad to be home, exhausted from the hot, steamy days at the ocean and pool, as well as long nights of eating, drinking, and having fun. I suppose my feelings can be defined with the present understanding that life needs to be lived with love, truth, forgiveness, and hope. I learned this from my family. I am fortunate. Yet coming together, *this* time, and witnessing signs that my brothers, sisters and I are no longer in the lush, green summers of our lives, and seeing our children as the young adults *we* once were, is sobering. Life here on earth is finite, and without warning we are old, must give in to limitations, and embrace what is, as we see Mom do. I am reminded that I am not my physical body—this biological compilation of bones, blood, tissue, and genetic components. I am soul, spirit, and an eternal energy that is perfect, divine, and never changes. Whether I am five, fifty, or eighty, I am eternally young and timeless. I am connected to all human beings by God's light. I am acutely aware at this moment, that in this lifetime I am connected irrevocably to my amazing family, not only by that light, but also by a deep and precious love for each and every member, simply because I choose to be. Burroughs love like no other. Burroughs' love is unwavering and unbreakable, formed and solidified by Mom and Dad, who showed us in the best way they knew how, what it means to love, and how to forgive. We learned well, and I think for the most part, we have passed this understanding on to our many children. Bravo for us!

"TIME IS AN ILLUSION FORMED BY
THE HUMAN OBSERVATION OF BIRTH,
AGING, AND DEATH
OF THE PHYSICAL FORM.
YET, SPIRIT/SOUL IS TIMELESS
AND EXISTS IN AN ETERNAL
PRESENT MOMENT."

"IN MY FAMILY, IT IS EFFORTLESS
TO LOVE ONE ANOTHER AND FOCUS
ON EACH OTHER'S STRENGTHS
BECAUSE WE HAVE LEARNED
TO HONOR OUR DIFFERENCES
AND ALWAYS BE WILLING TO FORGIVE."

# Grateful Love
## (Sam's Cardiac Catheterization)

Routine procedure
Gone terribly wrong—
Vessel was twisted,
Artery torn.

They said, "Only hours …
You'll be on your way"
But now they fear bleeding
And whisk him away.

Fear builds inside me;
He can't see me cry,
Can't see I'm trembling;
"God, tell me WHY"

Rushed to Stone River;
That hospital is best.
I follow in terror,
Surgery or test?

His vitals are stable,
Circulation is good;
We wait through the nighttime,
The pain he withstood.

I look in his eyes
Caressing his face,
Praying for a miracle,
Preparing in case.

I call all prayer warriors
Asking, "Please pray he heals."
Like torrents of rain
They pray; I believe.

The morning brings smiles;
His vessel has healed.
A test shows no blockage,
No bypass revealed.

The crisis is over;
Tears flow from my heart.
"You will be OK;
We won't be apart."

Gratitude gushes;
We embrace the day.
Our prayers have been answered,
Death taken away.

"AFTER A ROUTINE
DIAGNOSTIC HEART PROCEDURE,
I ALMOST LOST SAM.
THANK GOD WE HAVE
SO MANY PEOPLE WHO LOVE US
AND PRAYED FOR HIM.
PRAYER WARRIORS ROCK!"

# *Get Me to the Church on Time*

"OK, Sam," I announced. "We need a break. I need a break. We've been working our butts off for days, weeks, and months. I know that tomorrow everyone is coming into town for our wedding, and we still have so much to do, but right now I need to go down to the beach, and enjoy a few moments of relaxation. So get your bathing suit on, honey, and let's go, even if it's just for an hour."

"Sounds like a plan," Sam agreed. "Just give me one minute and I'll be ready to go."

The weather was magnificent. It was about 4:30 p.m. That brilliant, golden globe hung effortlessly in the cloudless, aqua sky. Sunset was still hours away, since it was mid-July. Though we could feel intense heat on our skin, there was scarcely a drop of moisture in the air, so we were comfortable and content envisioning spending the next few days with our family and friends, celebrating our wedding weekend together. We brought our beach chairs close to the water and faced them South towards the sun hoping to put a fresh, bronzed, look to our already tanned bodies so we would look our best for the big day.

We stayed a little over an hour, then packed up and headed back home. Once there, we continued with our house preparations. Sam was mowing the lawn, and I was sweeping the floor in the foyer by the front door. The wedding was to take place on Saturday. However, on Friday night we were having a gathering in our backyard for all of our family arriving early and staying at a local hotel. I could hear the sound of the mower in the background as I bent down with the dust pan and brush. Without warning, in a split second of horror, I heard and felt a loud pop, and immediately crashed helplessly and violently to the hard, tiled, floor. I could feel the head of the femur (the long bone in the thigh) sitting to the left of the acetabulum (the cup shaped socket), where a moment earlier it sat appropriately in place.

"Oh my God, not now; please, not now! This can't be happening," I shrieked. "Please make it go back in," I pleaded as intense, sharp unrelenting pain gripped my body sending muscles into acute spasm and causing neurons to explode in my brain.

One of my worst nightmares had happened. The prosthetic hip that was implanted nearly eight years ago had dislocated. It popped completely out of the socket and I lay helpless, immobilized, and in shock. I was on my back with my left leg bent. Straightening it was impossible due to the pathological, twisted anatomy that was now my stark reality. I had to bend the right leg and press my right knee forcefully against the left one to keep the left leg from flopping over, which I was certain would have sent my pain to even more intolerable levels and would have caused me to pass out. I couldn't pass out. I needed help.

"Sam," I screamed as loudly as I possibly could since I knew he would have to hear me above the roar of the lawn mower.

I continued screaming his name over and over, and thankfully he thought he heard something, so he cut the engine. It was a bloodcurdling screech that sent chills all the way through him. He knew something had to be terribly wrong. He flew into the house like a rocket and found me on the floor, writhing in pain.

"It's out, it's out, it's out," I moaned over and over. "Oh my God, Sam, not now; this can't be happening now. Please make it OK; make it go away. I can't stand the pain."

"Oh my God, Dru, what do I do?" Sam implored, knowing exactly what I was talking about.

"Call 911 now; call 911."

Sam frantically made the call and within a few minutes, police cars, an ambulance, and paramedics arrived.

"You can't touch me," I screamed. "You can't move me, please. The pain is too much. Oh my God, please! I'm getting married on Saturday. You have to fix this," I begged and at the same time refused to allow anyone to come anywhere near me.

"Ma'am, we have to get you onto the stretcher and to the hospital. We will try to be as gentle as we can but we have to move you."

I agreed with intense fear and trepidation. I had no choice. They tried to be gentle but every movement sent waves of intense unbearable pain that took my breath away and brought up guttural, anguished sounds I never thought I was capable of emitting.

"We're going to turn the lights and the sirens off," one of the paramedics informed me. "We will go very slowly but I have to warn you; the bumps and turns won't be easy."

He wasn't exaggerating. It was the longest ten minutes of my life. With every bump and turn I screamed, and then proceeded to apologize and moan, "I'm sorry. I'm not really like this." I kept repeating over and over that I was getting married in two days and pleaded with them to fix my hip. Of course, they couldn't. They were just a transport team, but I was far from rational at that point. After a particularly forceful jolt, I again screamed reaching desperately into the air above me for an invisible hand to clutch onto. In that wild excruciating moment one of the paramedics grabbed my hand.

"Squeeze it," he yelled loudly and adamantly. "Just squeeze it. It will help."

Once at the hospital, the doctor on staff took one look at me and told the nurses to get an IV in me and some pain meds as quickly as possible. It was amazing how fast the drugs took effect. I literally went from mid-scream to silence and a body that was limp, pain free, but feeling horribly out of control from the strong medication. The x-rays confirmed what I already knew. The hip was dislocated.

"Ms. Mainer, I'm Doctor Levendis. We need to manipulate your hip back into the socket. You can't be awake for it. The trauma and pain would be too great. So we need to give you an amnesia medication so you will not remember the trauma. Once we have completed the procedure we will then give you the anti-amnesia drug to bring you back. Is that OK with you?"

"Oh my God," I responded groggily and with speech that was slurred and barely audible. "You're messing with my brain. Please, I pleaded, Just tell me you can fix this."

"Look into my eyes," Doctor Levendis said sternly taking his index and middle fingers and pointing them directly at both of his eyes. "One hundred percent; I can fix this."

Sam reached down and took my hand. He had been my rock through the whole ordeal, telling me it would be OK even though he really didn't know at all if it would be. He was just as terrified as I was but he didn't show it. I gathered strength from his positive resolve and determined faith. The love in his eyes was undeniable as he told me again they would fix it, and we would have our beautiful wedding. I trusted him more than any of the doctors at that moment. I nodded my head giving the go-ahead.

With that, they injected the medication into the IV and I ventured to an ethereal place of incredible beauty, light, and peace. I could hear muffled voices in the background but I knew I was far away. I can't describe what this place looked like. It was more of a feeling of intense love and joy rather than a distinct vision. There was no pain, no fear, only contentment, and I was enveloped by a magnificent, brilliant light. The next thing I remember is seeing the face of one of the nurses coming slowly back into focus.

"Oh, it's you, "I cooed sleepily. "I think I just went to heaven."

"Okaaaaay," she sung warily and smiled, clearly letting me know that she believed that my sojourn to that heavenly place was merely the effect of the strong medication I was given.

"No really," I insisted. "I really think I went to heaven."

"Mom, are you OK," Brianne implored as she reached down and hugged me, obviously very worried.

My other daughter Allison was there too and Bri's boyfriend Brett as well. I was so happy to see them and I think Sam was too. It had been quite a nightmare for him and he appreciated their support.

"I'm OK, I think," I responded. "I'm so glad you guys are here. I just want to go home."

I looked down at my legs and they were lying straight out in front of me so I knew the procedure had been a success. Cooling waves of glorious relief washed gently over me. "Maybe we were getting married after all," I mused!

"A PERSON'S TRUE CHARACTER
IS OFTEN TESTED
AND SOMETIMES REVEALED
DURING TIMES OF INTENSE ADVERSITY.
MY HUSBAND IS MY INSPIRATION,
ALWAYS CONSISTENT, GENUINE,
LOVING, AND SUPPORTIVE
EVERY MOMENT OF EVERY DAY,
EVEN IN A CRISIS.
THANK YOU, SAM."

# *Uncovered Gemstone*

Sleep slowly faded into the backdrop of dawn's luminescence. It was a glorious day evident by the shafts of glistening sunlight filtering through the blinds. Those soft, golden rays of early morning reflected mystical, lifelike shadows cast by the swaying branches of sleepy trees that now danced on the walls of our bedroom. Memories of the previous night's horror began creeping back into my mind. I felt a twinge of pain in my arm where the IV had been. I remembered, in my drug induced stupor, having had to rip it out myself when we got home from the hospital because the nurses in the ER, in all the confusion, forgot. I tried to move and felt a dull aching in my hip where the head of the prosthesis had been manipulated back into place.

"Oh my God, it's Friday the day before our wedding," I thought with mixed feelings of excitement and consternation. "I hope I can walk. I wonder if I can dance. Who in the world will be able to bring the enormous amount of supplies to the wedding site if I can't?"

The Village Center, in the town we live in, is where the ceremony and the reception were to take place. The only things provided to us were the space, the tables and chairs, two kitchens, and a bird's eye, panoramic, picturesque view of Long Island Sound. We had rented a good amount of items from a caterer including linen, chafing dishes, champagne and wine glasses, coffee urns, etc., and were utilizing a local restaurant to supply the dinner. Other than that, Sam and I had to haul everything up to the third floor: 15 cases of wine, 15 cases of beer, all cooking and serving supplies, food to be cooked and served at the cocktail hour, 150 wedding cupcakes made by my daughters, trays of cookies, and other pastries, not to mention a slew of other decorations and incidentals so the affair would be unique and elegant. On top of all that, we had a window of an hour and a half to transform the barren catering hall into the magical, fairy tale wedding we had envisioned. We had hired a wait staff, but before they could even begin to do their job, we had to prepare the space.

First things first, however, I had been sent home from the hospital with a long brace that went from my hip to my ankle and strict instructions that I was to see an orthopedist first thing in the morning to determine if it would be alright for me to walk, much less dance at my wedding.

I slowly stepped onto the floor and realized that putting pressure on my leg didn't seem to cause too much pain. I was encouraged. I slowly made my way downstairs and called the orthopedist to see if I could get in that morning. Even though it was Friday and the wedding wasn't until Saturday, we had a rather large gathering of family and friends who had gotten into town early, coming to our house later that evening. We had a million things to do but we also knew there was a chance that none of it would happen. I never really believed that. I was certain the doctor would not say the wedding was off, and luckily, I was correct. He told me to take it easy and be very careful. I could walk and better yet, I could dance, brace-free.

As soon as my brothers and sisters found out what happened, the phone began to ring.

"Oh my God," my sister Sara screamed into the phone half laughing but also revealing genuine concern. "Weren't you already the center of attention?"

"I know," I quipped giggling. "I'll do anything to brighten the spotlight."

And so began our magnificent wedding weekend. I was in a

considerable amount of pain and unable to do much to help Sam. The party on Friday night wasn't too big a deal. Sam had made a big pot of chili a few days before. We ordered some three-foot-long sandwiches from a deli and a good friend made some terrific salads. Of course, there was plenty of cold beer and spirits to satisfy everyone's palate. It was a glorious, comfortable, summer evening, and I was reveling in the fact that I had my entire family with me for our big day. Later that night, after my family had gone back to the hotel, Sam's family began filtering into the backyard including Sam's sons, their wives, and our grandchildren. We were all primed and ready for a grand celebration.

Saturday morning made an entrance in much the same way Friday did. For months I fought the tendency to agonize over whether we would have the magnificent sunset I had jokingly ordered up special from the staff at the Village Center. On July 16, 2011, the sky was cloudless with nary a drop of humidity in the air and the unfiltered sun enhanced all of the brilliant, vibrant colors of that gorgeous midsummer day. I don't think I ever remember a more beautiful day in our quaint little port town. The angels were shining their light on us, and I was certain we would have our dream wedding. The only problem was, how were we going to get all that stuff to the Village Center at 1:00 p.m., set up the ceremony downstairs, the cocktail hour and reception upstairs, and be showered, dressed, and ready by 4:00 p.m.? I wondered what we had been thinking. Even if I wasn't injured, I don't think we could have managed it.

I didn't wallow in my fears and apprehension for long. The phone rang again.

"Dru, it's Sara again," announced my sister. "We will meet you and Sam at the Village Center at 1:00 p.m. Everyone will be there: brothers and sisters, spouses and kids. You just tell us what to do and we'll do it.

Don't worry. It will get done."

I pressed my hand against my heart and closed my eyes. Tears spilled from beneath them as thoughts of Company "B" came flooding into my mind. In an odd "out of body" experience I saw different scenes from my life. In an instant, I reminisced and relived all of those crazy, chaotic, confusing times as a child. I remembered how insignificant I felt among so many siblings and how I fought to fit in and be different at the same time. I thought about how long it had taken for me to figure out who I was, apart from my family, and as an individual. I even thought about the time when I was a young woman, and I had pushed my family away thinking there must be something better out there.

"Dru, are you there? Did you hear me," Sara questioned.

"Yeah, Sara," I said, my voice cracking. Choking back the tears, I continued "I don't know what to say. Thank you, thank you; thank you. I'll see you later."

At exactly 1:00 p.m. a focused, determined troop of people descended on the Village Center. It took at least ten trips with large rolling tables filled to the brim to haul the supplies to the third floor. The guys began ripping open cases of beer and bags of ice, and filled large plastic barrels. Everyone started asking what they should do.

"Round table cloths in this room and oval ones in the other," I barked joyfully. "Here are the table cards and the diagram of the reception room showing where they go and how many people are at each table. Wine and champagne glasses are to be placed to the right of the place setting. This is the way I need the turquoise, linen napkins folded, chafing dishes here, dessert table there."

So it went. Two sets of neighbors, who had created centerpieces made from gorgeous blue and white hydrangeas, were there as well, putting the final touches on our lovely affair. I watched with amazement as it all came together. I have never felt so genuinely loved in all my life. What had started as, what I thought was a tragedy two nights before, turned out to be a great, unexpected gift. I always believed my family loved me. After all, Mom said we had to love each other. However, that day I experienced their love in a personal, intimate way. I will never forget, and will carry and cherish that sweet memory always. Feeling so humbled, grateful, and intensely moved by their genuine and unconditional love for me—Dru—was a defining moment in my life. We had been raised as a unit, a team, Company "B," and in that moment we all moved together like a well-oiled machine, each doing their part to make a miracle happen, my miracle, our miracle, and the greatest wedding gift I received.

As I write this story, I am finding it difficult to find appropriate words that reflect my thoughts, feelings, and emotions. Perhaps, because moments like these are so deeply soul-filled and irradiated by the glorious light of all that is divinely perfect, and the way the world was meant to be, that human communication, words or even gestures are incapable of expressing it. Yet, I am guided by my heart and urged through my soul to try. I hope it is enough, and it adequately expresses my love and thanks to *my* Company "B."

"IN THE MIDST OF UNFORESEEN
MOMENTS OF PAIN AND SUFFERING,
IT IS HARD TO BELIEVE
THERE MAY BE A HIDDEN TREASURE
BURIED WITHIN IT.
MY WONDERFUL WEDDING EXPERIENCE
REMINDS ME TO BELIEVE THAT
EVERYTHING HAPPENS
FOR A REASON AND
THE LIGHT OF DAWN MAY
REVEAL THAT UNEXPECTED GIFT."

# *Always Only You*
### (My Wedding Vows to Sam)

It all started with a single kiss,
A moment of magic, a moment of bliss.
You opened my heart and poured forth your soul
And quickly our love began to unfold.

I came to know you and I was deeply in awe
Of the peace and serenity I continuously saw.
You showed me a love I had never known;
Since that time, our love has blossomed and grown.

I imagined my prince on a horse of pure white.
You came on a stallion made of metal and pipes,
We flew like the wind to a place of romance;
We loved, we laughed, we cried, and we danced.

In the quiet moments of the early dawn
I look up to the heavens and thank God you were born.
I am grateful for the time He has given us to share.
I promise to always, treat your heart with care.

Our love is timeless, celestial, and divine;
I am certain we'll be one 'til the end of time.
In this special moment I give you my soul,
Hand in hand together, we'll live and grow old.

With this ring I promise to tend to your wings
So that you can always fly free, and follow your dreams.
I promise to teach you truths I learn on my way;
Please share your wisdom at the end of each day.

With each glorious sunset and each silvery moon,
With each sparkling snowfall and each flower that blooms,
I will love you, and cherish you, and hold you tight,
And today through eternity I will always be your wife.

# *Woman*

*(Sam's Wedding Vows to Me, Written by Sam)*

She's found herself and walks her path;
Her words are strong and true.
Her eyes … they speak of love and peace;
Her smile will waken you.

She laughs at life but understands
The meaning of it all.
She'll do a shot and sing a song
But cry when children fall.

Sometimes she's like a little girl
Who needs a stronger hand;
She snuggles in and feels secure
And wants me as a man.

She's felt the pain of emptiness
And dreams that flew away,
But through it all she listened hard,
And learned to bless each day.

We talk of things that matter most,
Of why and how and God,
But never lose the thrill of now …
She beckons with a nod.

My woman shows me who she is;
She's not afraid to bleed.
She aches and cries and laughs and loves,
And conquers every need.

She shows me when I've gone astray
Without a judging mind.
She helps me find my way again;
She's gentle and she's kind.

We'll feel the days when we're apart
And dream of our return.
But celebrate each other's soul ...
To live, to look, to learn.

And so my love, come live with me;
Let's drink of life's sweet wine.
We'll wake each morn' with hearts on fire
And gaze at the divine.

# *A Peak Through the Portal*

*L*ife, indeed, is full of adversity. I know that not many people would question that. Though most of us have abundant blessings, I have never met anyone who has escaped the challenges of dealing with life's losses, disappointments, and defeats. I have learned over the years, as most of these stories illustrate, that it isn't about the adversity that presents itself in my life, but how I choose to handle it. I can ask the useless question "why me?" and wallow in self-pity. I can opt to blame other people, God, or the world for my suffering, or on the other hand, I can choose to embrace it. As I have explained, I have come to understand that I draw circumstances into my life, good and unpleasant, to learn lessons. If I ignore the lesson, it will continue to present itself over and over in the form of different experiences until I finally turn, face it, and determine what it is I am being called upon to learn.

As you have seen, I have had my share of adversity. Some of it was the result of poor choices I made; for example marrying a difficult, fearful, angry man. My struggles during that time led me on a deep spiritual path in an attempt to find some understanding as to why I had created such a horrific situation. The years of trying to extricate myself from the marriage and distance myself from Jake, were obviously difficult, frightening, and challenging. Trying to help myself and my three children heal in the aftermath of the horrendous, destructive, custody war left little time for dwelling on what had just happened to all of us. I often wondered if I had adequately dealt with it, or not. In one unexpected moment, would it come rushing upward and outward from that deep sacred chamber where I had hidden it all away?

During a deep meditation years ago, I had a profound experience and an intense vision. I saw in my mind's eye a staircase lit on one side of the wall by candles—the colors of the rainbow or the seven chakras. It descended downward to an unknown space. I was accompanied by a beautiful angelic being and upon its gentle urging I began to take one step at a time down the long stairwell.

Uneasiness and apprehension began to envelop me. I was terrified that I had found that secret space where I believed I had buried all of my pain and trauma.

"Turn and run," screamed a voice inside my head as the terrifying feelings and emotions got stronger and stronger. "Don't go there. You don't know what will happen if you open that door. You may never recover from having to relive all of it all over again."

Once more, at the urging of my spirit friend, I gathered the courage and brought forth the trust I needed to face my past. Upon reaching the bottom of the stairs, I slowly and with much trepidation, turned the knob, feeling my heart pound and my entire body tremble. I carefully pushed the door ajar, just a bit, and peered around the corner. I was shocked! What I saw was not at all what I had expected! It was the most beautiful, lush, fragrant garden I had ever seen. The varieties of blooms included some that were completely unfamiliar to me. The colors were so intense and bright, and the hues didn't match the spectrum of colors we have available to us in this earthly realm. There was a heavenly light coming from an unknown origin that made everything sparkle like diamonds and it filled the air with warmth.

I opened the door wider and entered with spirit companion by my side.

"What is this beautiful, amazing place?" I questioned.

"It is the mystical, unearthly garden that you have created through your love and good works," my guide responded. "It exists in the very core of all souls and defines its level of spiritual growth, and awareness. The garden of the eternal soul flourishes most by overcoming adversity with love and forgiveness committing itself to an unwavering intension to grow more radiant despite life's difficulties, and to use that illumination to help others."

"Each flower in your garden," she continued, "represents one of the painful moments in your life. The seed from each adversity was planted in the rich, fertile soil of your divine soul. It then received life-giving moisture from the anguished, sorrowful tears you shed during the darkest moments of your days. The illumination of your soul, generated by the selfless acts of love and kindness you bestowed upon others, provided the most necessary ingredient, *light.* The soft petals reached upward toward that light each time you chose to *BE Love.*' Your garden grew and flourished through the many heartfelt prayers of hope you shared, faith you proclaimed, and gratitude you offered. The otherworldly melodies and symphonies that waft softly through the air are the angels giving music to your words."

Tears were now falling gently from my joyful heart as I realized that my past was indeed buried deep inside me just as I had thought. However, the pain, sadness, and sorrow had been transformed into beauty, light, and love. Though much of the time it was a struggle, my ability to embrace life's adversities, and find the gift or the treasure buried within all of them was the secret that allowed this transformation to be possible. Though I choose now to do everything in my power to grow from joy instead of adversity by making better choices, I know that when I am asked to face another difficult circumstance, I envision my magical, mystical garden. I imagine another tiny, miraculous seed that will take root, germinate and grow into a beautiful, fragrant, colorful flower. I know that my soul's garden will continue to flourish and become even lovelier, and I will be forever and overwhelmingly grateful for all of my life.

Dhanyavad! (Thank you!)

# Sharing My Soul's Garden with You

I traveled deep inside myself
To a tiny darkened room.
It holds my pain from yesterday,
And I guard it like a sacred tomb.

I wonder why I locked it away
Instead of letting it go.
I don't remember what's inside
But it's time, and I need to know.

I notice a room in the distance,
And suddenly I am filled with fear.
What if the pain is too much to bear?
There's so much from so many years.

I stand for what seems like forever
Holding a key made of light and truth;
It was given to me by the angels
Long ago, in my innocent youth.

I slowly and carefully open the door
And hesitantly walk inside.
At first all I see is darkness
Until I look with my inner eyes.

I am immediately struck with wonder;
It is not what I expected to see.
All around me, a landscape of beauty,
My spirit feels peaceful and free.

In this room is a beautiful garden,
Every pain, now a lovely flower;
All the tears I shed helped them to grow
Gently falling like a warm April shower.

Each time I learned from adversity
My garden was more filled with life.
The light of my soul was its sunshine;
Its food was my trials and strife.

As I look at the majesty before me
I can see how much I have grown.
I am thankful for all of my suffering
And this miracle I have been shown.

Perhaps, I would never have discovered
This beautiful magical place
If so many had not come into my life
And shared their soul's embrace.

So I invite you into my garden;
Lie gently down by the stream.
Let the scent of the flowers consume you
As you close your eyes and dream.

"I TRULY BELIEVE
THAT BY SHARING WITH EACH OTHER
OUR SACRED LIFE STORIES,
OUR DISCOVERED WISDOM,
AND OUR REMEMBERED TRUTH,
WE WILL SURELY BECOME
A UNIFYING FORCE
FOR DIVINE LOVE
AND OUR PRECIOUS WORLD
WILL FINALLY KNOW REAL PEACE.
I BELIEVE!"

# Conclusion

*A* nd so, *Treasures of the Soul* was sent to my publisher, Legwork Team Publishing. I am beyond excited, and I look forward to what I hope will be, the beginning of many new and enlightening relationships as our paths cross through the reading of this book. It has been a wonderful experience, sharing my life and my heart with all of you. I urge you, once again, to remember that we are all spiritual partners on a path. As eternal souls and human beings, we are all connected by one, loving energy, our Creator, God, Mohammad, Allah, our Higher Power, or whatever you choose to call it. Together, as we tap into this wonderful unifying power, we can all make a tremendous difference in the world. We can choose to remember our innate, loving nature and live our lives with only one prayer, "Please, God, help me to *BE LOVE!*" For me, understanding and embracing that individual concept helps me to look beyond a person's shortcomings, dysfunction or negativity, and see the Divinity within them.

Far too often we have a tendency, in the heat of the moment or when our lives are in turmoil and we are suffering, to react to a situation or person from the vantage point of the frightened wounded child, the ego. Many times, during my life, I have fallen prey to that insecure, doubtful part of me. When I did, and I listened to the advice or urgings that came from that fearful place, I inevitably made less than perfect choices, which led me down difficult and treacherous paths. Of course, there really are no mistakes or failures, only lessons to be learned. The goal is to begin being able to differentiate between the wise and enlightened voices of our souls,

## Conclusion

God, angels and our guides, and that of our frightened ego-self. Once we have accomplished this, we will choose more wisely and find ourselves learning much more through joy than through adversity.

That said, if we find ourselves still occupying space in this earthly classroom, it means that we have not learned all of our lessons and our work here is not complete. Life will always present its challenges and opportunities to choose love over hate, compassion over judgment, forgiveness over vengeance, etc. Being human allows us to feel deeply and experience human emotions in a way not available to us in spirit. Along with those emotions come choices about how we will respond ... rather react to life's challenges. When we pause in those moments of confusion, sadness or suffering, and listen quietly to the still, quiet voices of Divine guidance, we are reminded again and again that all things, even suffering, have purpose. All of life can be embraced with joy and acceptance knowing that each experience will bring us closer to the full remembrance of our authentic divine self.

Remembering and consistently reminding ourselves that God creates only love and magnificence helps us not only see majesty in ourselves, but in all others as well. Observing and encountering individuals who are behaving in ways that do not reflect qualities of the soul will also remind us, that if they were in touch, in the present moment with their divine self, they could not behave in ways opposed to Spirit. With this understanding, we will be guided to respond with great compassion, forgiveness and love. This awareness does not mean that we should allow anyone to abuse or victimize us. It does allow us to release any individual who does so, with love and a sincere prayer that he or she may awaken and remember his or her true, loving and beautiful soul.

I will now say goodbye, until we meet again, as you, hopefully, share

264

your stories with me. I am anxious to enter your classroom and hear about things that you have learned through your own travels. As I have said, I believe that in addition to learning our lessons and working through our karma we also have an obligation to offer our gifts and share what we have learned. I have been blessed with many teachers in my life from both the physical world and the world of spirit. I am grateful to be able to give the gift of *Treasures of the Soul* to this world. I hope that within its pages you, my readers, will find even the tiniest spark to ignite within you a fire that will help you remember your greatness and illuminate your truth.

The Blessed and wondrous Divinity in me recognizes and appreciates the same within you.

*Namaste,*

*Drusilla*

# About the Author

**Drusilla Burrough,** LMT is a licensed massage therapist who has been working in the Long Island, New York area for the last fifteen years. Her work in the field as well as her difficult life circumstances have led her to rely on the ever-consistent and loving assistance from her spirit guides, the angelic kingdom, and her wise, enlightened higher self. She has developed amazing gifts of spiritual sensitivity and an ability to reach beyond the earthly veil to that, which can't be seen, felt, or heard with our physical senses. Her beautiful writing style and unique content sends an underlying, and forthright message to her readers and clients that "we are all magnificent beings of divine light and love," created in a beautiful perfection that cannot be fully understood and embraced without remembering our authentic "divine self." She has dedicated her life and career to helping those who cross her path remember how magnificent they are, and that they are absolutely, without question, *"beautiful, powerful, spiritual beings, having a human experience."* She urges us to remember that it is the beautiful soul or "God Part" of us all that can create miraculous wonders in our lives. She believes it is her mission to deliver this message, and in turn, those enlightened souls who do *"remember"* will then go forth and help others to do the same, and together we can truly bring heaven to earth and peace on earth.

# Treasures of the Soul

If you have any questions, thoughts or prayer requests, or if you would
like to share your own stories of adversity and struggles or mystical tales
of love, light, and inspiration, please email Drusilla Burrough at
drusilla@treasuresofthesoulbooks.com or visit her website:
www.treasuresofthesoulbooks.com

Additional copies of this book may be purchased online from
www.LegworkTeam.com; www.Amazon.com;
www.BarnesandNoble.com; or via the author's website:
www.treasuresofthesoulbooks.com

You can also obtain a copy of the book by visiting
L.I. Books Bookstore
80 Davids Drive, Suite One, Hauppauge, NY 11788
or by ordering it from your favorite bookstore.

CPSIA information can be obtained at www.ICGtesting.com
Printed in the USA
BVOW011409140512

290014BV00006B/2/P